Judo in the U.S.

Judo in the U.S.

A Century
of
Dedication

**Michel Brousse
and David Matsumoto**

PREFACE BY RYOZO KATO
AMBASSADOR OF JAPAN TO THE U.S.A.

NORTH ATLANTIC BOOKS
BERKELEY, CALIFORNIA

Published by
The United States Judo Federation
P.O. Box 338
Ontario, OR 97914-0338

and

North Atlantic Books
P.O. Box 12327
Berkeley, California 94712

Cover photograph by David Finch
Archival cover photographs courtesy of the
    University of California, Berkeley, and the
    Judo Black Belt Association of Hawaii
Cover design by Brad Greene
Text design by Bernard Delcros
Printed in Singapore
Distributed to the book trade by Publishers
    Group West

Judo in the U.S.: A Century of Dedication has been made possible in part by the generous contributions of Hatashita International, Signature Associates–ONCOR International, and Snyder, Kinney, Bennett & Keating, Inc. We thank them for helping us celebrate judo practice in the U.S. by commemorating the USJF's fiftieth anniversary with this book.

Judo in the U.S.: A Century of Dedication is sponsored by the Society for the Study of Native Arts and Sciences, a nonprofit educational corporation whose goals are to develop an educational and crosscultural perspective linking various scientific, social, and artistic fields; to nurture a holistic view of arts, sciences, humanities, and healing; and to publish and distribute literature on the relationship of mind, body, and nature.

North Atlantic Books' publications are available through most bookstores. For further information, call 800-337-2665 or visit our website at www.northatlanticbooks. com. Substantial discounts on bulk quantities are available to corporations, professional associations, and other organizations. For details and discount information, contact our special sales department.

Library of Congress Cataloging-in-Publication Data

Brousse, Michel.
    Judo in the U.S. : a century of dedication / by Michel
Brousse and David Matsumoto.
        p. cm.
    Includes bibliographical references.
    ISBN 1-55643-563-0 (pbk.)
    1. Judo—United States—History. I. Matsumoto, David Ricky.
II. Title.
    GV1114.B75 2005
    796.815'2'0973—dc22
                                            2005010774
                                            CIP

1 2 3 4 5 6 7 8 9 TWP 10 09 08 07 06 05

This book is dedicated

to

Fanny Brousse and Sayaka Matsumoto
for their undying support, contributions to judo,
and the joy they bring to our lives

The pioneers and all those who today dedicate their lives
to Judo in America

PREFACE

The year 2003 marks the 150th anniversary of Commodore Matthew Perry's arrival in Japan. Over the course of these 150 years, one cannot help but marvel at how the friendship between the two countries has matured and how Judo has been able to play a role in creating an environment where the relationship continues to blossom.

Judo's establishment as an authentic national martial art would not have been possible without the influence of one very special individual, Master Jigoro Kano, the founder of the Kodokan in Japan. (On a personal note, Master Kano was the matchmaker between my father, who was also a judo player, and my mother.)

Master Kano started Judo at a time when Japan had secluded itself from the rest of the world "sakoku." But he was not a narrow-minded nationalist. He was a forward-looking individual who after firmly establishing Judo in Japan, hoped to promote Judo on a global basis. In fact, Master Kano became the first Asian member of the International Olympic Committee in 1909 and he was indefatigable in working to spread Judo to a worldwide audience.

As a result of Master Kano's tireless efforts, Judo became the first of the traditional martial arts to break out from the confines of Japan and become popular in the United States and other countries. Its debut as an official sport at the 1964 Tokyo Olympics forever cemented its status as an international sport and provided an opportunity for the world to revel in its combination of beauty and strength. If Master Kano were alive today, he would be very pleased to see the international acceptance of the sport.

While I applaud the growing popularity of the sport, my one small regret is the increased emphasis on winning versus concentrating on technique and style. Winning should not be the sole objective; it should be linked to fair play and follow the original principles that were laid down by Master Kano.

Taking advantage of your opponent's strengths is what makes Judo such a tremendous sport. It rewards flexibility over sheer strength or put another way, it allows "the soft way" to triumph over toughness. Unlike American football, where there is a clearly defined difference between offense and defense, Judo is a combination of both of these influences. This blending of influences, like the blending of our two cultures, makes Judo a perfect bridge between the United States and Japan.

Most importantly, the success of Judo has also led to the deepening and strengthening of the friendship between the United States and Japan. The cultures of the two countries have increasingly become intertwined. In this day and age, one can just as easily get burgers in Tokyo as one can get sushi in Cleveland. Americans do not think twice about driving Japanese cars while the Japanese cannot get enough of American made movies.

On that score, two individuals who richly deserve special mention are Dr. David R. Matsumoto and Professor Michel Brousse. These two have undertaken the task of exploring this melding of cultures and also exploring Judo's influence on the culture and history of both the United States and Japan. This book sheds light on the history of Judo's initial development in Japan and the United States. It also provides important insight into how two very diverse cultures can learn from each other for their mutual enrichment, and how this process has cemented the friendship and goodwill between the two nations.

This book will certainly find an honored place on the bookshelves of Judo devotees, but I am equally convinced that its insights will also have broad appeal to students of international relations.

Ryozo Kato　　加藤良三

Ambassador of Japan to the United States of America

UNITED STATES
JUDO FEDERATION
FOUNDED 1952

UNITED STATES JUDO FEDERATION

President
Noboru Saito

Mailing Address:	**Telephone:**	**Faxes:**	**Internet:**
P. O. Box 338	(541) 889-8753	(541) 889-5836	www.usjf.com
Ontario, OR 97914-0338		(413) 502-4983	no@usjf.com

On the occasion of the Fiftieth Anniversary of the United States Judo Federation (USJF), the USJF commissioned this historical book *Judo in the U.S.: A Century of Dedication.* The purpose of this book is to preserve our rich Judo heritage in the United States of America, to honor our Judo pioneers, and to collect historical Judo data for safekeeping for the generations to come.

When I was elected to the presidency of the USJF in April 2000, I felt there was a need to keep an accurate history of American Judo, especially by recording certain significant events, such as the breakup of the United States Judo Association from the United States Judo Federation and the formation of the AAU Judo Committee, as well as the passage of the Olympic Sports Act in 1979 and the creation of United States Judo, Inc. This book accomplishes that goal.

In understanding our history, we will gain insight into many questions about the future of Judo in the years ahead: Why do we have three national organizations? Where are we going from here? Can we progress? Can we find a common ground and work together to make American Judo grow? Does the American public know that Judo is different from Karate?

To the best of my knowledge, this book is the first Judo book of this magnitude to be published by an American Judo organization. I hope this will contribute to the recognition and understanding of Judo in America.

My sincere appreciation goes to both Dr. David Matsumoto and Prof. Michel Brousse for taking on the enormous task of writing this book. I know that without their talented writing skills and their dedication to work hard, despite their busy schedules, this book could not be realized. I am very fortunate to have our USJF Executive Committee and the Board of Directors that are willing to take the chance to publish this book. I also am grateful to our members and other supporters of Judo, who gave generous donations to this project. We could not have done it without your contributions. Thank you very much.

Many people also helped by supplying historical pictures, articles, stories, anecdotes, and other contributions. Among them, the Kodokan Institute's cooperation was essential to gathering the dates for this book. Mr. Yukimitsu Kano (President), Mr. Naoki Murata (Kodokan Library), and his staff gave us tremendous help. Without their assistance, we could not have completed this project. "Domo taihen arigato gozaimashita."

I am proud of our accomplishment in producing this Judo history book and of the rich Judo history it records. Once again, I extend my sincere congratulations and appreciation to both Dr. Matsumoto and Prof. Brousse.

Happy Fiftieth Anniversary to the United States Judo Federation! I am looking forward to a prosperous future for our great organization.

Noboru Saito *Noboru Saito*

President, United States Judo Federation

ACKNOWLEDGMENTS

This book has been a long time in the making and would not have been possible without the help of many people. It is a pleasure to thank them. This book was meant to celebrate the 50th anniversary of the United States Judo Federation. The authors express their gratitude to President Saito and the USJF Executive Committee and the Board of Directors for their unfailing help and support.

This book is the result of long research that could not have been possible without the contribution of the judo family. In particular, we have received invaluable assistance from USJF President Noboru Saito. This book benefited from the expertise and kindness of the professional staffs at the archives that were visited. In gathering much of the material we are indebted to Kano Yukimitsu, head of the Kodokan Judo Institute, who granted us permission to examine and quote from their priceless collections of rare and unpublished archives. Murata Naoki, the curator, and his assistant, Morita Kikuko, have widely opened the doors of the Kodokan Library. We are deeply grateful to Robert C. Brink, Esq., for his helpful readings of the manuscript at a late stage of revision. We are also grateful for the comments of the people who generously shared sources and research leads and helped us to make this work more accurate and readable. Rusty Kanokogi, Nancy Kyoko Oda, Emilio Bruno, Jerry Hays, and Jason Morris deserve our best thanks for their large contribution.

Other people were very helpful in their field of expertise. They shared their knowledge, time, talent, and souvenirs during many interviews, and offered us their archives. We are very proud of the trust they put in us. We are deeply indebted to them: Edgar Allen, Jr., Dr. Mel Appelbaum, George Arrington, John Bassano, Jim Bregman, Ed Burgess, Lou DiGesare, Thomas Feldman, David Finch, Fukuda Keiko, Robert Fukuda, Fukusawa Aiko, Frank Fullerton, Esq., Constance Halporn, Gary Hashimoto, Sam Hashimoto, Carl Hayes, Wey Seng Kim, Billie Jean King, Gerald Lafon, David Long, Dr. Kei Narimatsu, Hayward Nishioka, Henry Ogawa, Roberta Park, Peter Perazio, Dr. Richard Riehle, Sakai Yoshitaro, Jeannie Schultz, Hal Sharp, Robert W. Smith, Robert Svinth, Sami Tadehara, Teri Takemori, Jan Todd, Jim Webb, Bob Willingham, Julia Bellrose Wynn, Harold Yamada, and Bob Young.

This book was financially supported by the USJF, by donors, and by sponsors. Without their generosity this work could not have been completed.

We offer special thanks to Sayaka Matsumoto, who served as our research assistant, aiding in the search for figures, photos, and illustrations; and to Françoise Brousse, who read and corrected countless drafts of the manuscript. We are also very pleased to thank institutions that helped us and gave us access to their archives: The IOC/Olympic Museum Collection; Black Belt Magazine; The Hirasaki National Resource Center of the Japanese American National Museum; The Japanese Americans Centennial Committee; The Buddhist Churches of America; The May Hill Museum; Ringling Bros. and Barnum & Bailey; The Todd-MacLean Physical Culture Collection of The University of Texas, Austin; The University of Washington Press; Popular Science Magazine, a division of Time4 Media, Inc.; DC Comics; Kiku Masamune, Sake Brewing Co. Ltd.; The Jerome Robbins Dance Division of The New York Public Library for Performing Arts, Astor, Lenox and Tilden Foundations; The Bancroft Library of the University of California, Berkeley; The Playboy Magazine; Tribune Media Services; PEANUTS © by Charles Schultz, United Feature Syndicate, Inc.; Black Cat © Lorne-Harvey Publications.

Special thanks to Bernard Delcros, who designed the layout for this book, and to Yvonne Cárdenas and the team at North Atlantic Books.

Although we are indebted to these fine individuals and institutions for their wonderful aid, any errors in the book are ours and ours alone.

Note: In this book individuals' names are usually presented with surnames following the given name. However, Japanese names are presented in the traditional Asian order with family name first.

CONTENTS

INTRODUCTION

Judo has gained a proper status in the world of American sports. Even though the Japanese method of fighting has been known to the American public since the early days of the 20th century, for long it has been kept on the margins of the U.S. sport culture because of its cultural roots. Over the last decades, judo as an Olympic sport has crowned American players. Larger audiences of U.S. sports fans and the media have gradually shown more interest. The brilliant victories of U.S. male and female elite players who won medals in the Olympic and World events have proved the quality of American judo and the maturity of its structures. In spite of this, a certain degree of confusion exists among the general public between judo and other martial arts. Self-defense, sport, and character building are entwined in the cultural representations of the masses. The image of the judo player has been for a vast majority of non-specialists a curious combination of dangerous skills, self-control, and sport trophies. A look at history will allow us to understand the key points of its development in this country.

The first problem faced by the historian is the definition of the subject of his study. What is judo? What are the relationships between judo and jujutsu? Today, judo's sport orientation makes clear the differences between the method of education founded in 1882 by Kano Jigoro and the combat techniques developed by samurai. Such a difference was not obvious in the early 1900s. A simple glance at the newspapers or at the dictionaries of those days is enough to see how undifferentiated the two practices were at the time. The emphasis Kano and his assistants laid on self-defense is another proof if necessary of the desire of the pioneers to take advantage of the jujutsu vogue in the Western countries.

What is implied by "practicing judo"? Here two perspectives have to be distinguished, one individual, the other social. As an individual practice, the Japanese method builds up its specificity upon three "pillars": self-defense, Oriental philosophy, and sport efficiency. Amazingly, judo practitioners do not view these three diverse elements as contradictory trends but as fundamental tenets giving coherence to their game.

The difficulty for the historian now is to face the wealth of meanings, and their evolution according to the places, to the people, and to the periods involved. Self-defense appears as the most important motivation for judo practitioners. Real or fake, the degree of invincibility promised by the advertisers of the Japanese method of fighting questions the reasons for such propaganda. Is or was U.S. society dangerous to the point that self-protection was needed for everyone? Or, could we speak of a "merchandizing of fear"? These questions have to be solved because they are related to the rooting of the image of jujutsu in the U.S. The discovery of Japan's civilization, of its culture and military prowess, has brought into relief new concepts and ways of life. Physical activities linking the improvement of mind and body have opened up new perspectives. Judo's sport orientation is evidence of Western influence. Interestingly, the shift from a martial art to a modern sport did not raise questions as long as the "modernization" of the art did not unbalance traditional values.

As a social activity, judo practice corresponds to a complex set of attitudes and behaviors meant to cement the judo subculture. Actually, as a subculture, judo is considered a sum of rules and rites that allows everyone to identify with the group and to distinguish a judo player as a member of the U.S. judo world. To be a *judoka* means to follow the codes, to accept hierarchy, to respect symbols, and to be faithful to the judo values originally defined by Kano, that is, discipline, courage, friendship, and respect. This brief analysis of the subject of study aims at justifying the choice of cultural history as the methodology for this study. In the U.S., judo was a cultural import. It was successively integrated then altered by American society. In order to understand the process and the steps of this evolution, the emphasis was put on values, forms, signs, and symbols. Instead of looking for the elements of causality, we have analyzed the structures, organizing collective usages, representations, and habits.

Because of this, the main sources we had to rely on are taken from the daily lives of American citizens. Cultural evidences of the Japanese method in the wide sense have been searched and studied for what they meant for the general public. A large number of fields were investigated: sport, physical education, but also art, entertainment, military, and police programs. Only a small part of it has been exhumed. Judo like many other sports has no recorded history. Oral stories are commonly used to revive the past and most of the time these stories are somewhat biased and often strictly intended to praise the pioneers.

Hierarchy in judo is a serious obstacle for the historian. Notwithstanding, the methods of oral history have been used to collect memories and many people contributed by sharing their pasts, allowing us to edit archives they treasured. However, the historical contribution of an individual cannot be equated with his desires. It is necessary to consider the role played by judo pioneers as a contribution within a wider system of influences.

Chapter one is an introduction to the method founded by Kano Jigoro to explain how previous combat techniques were merged into a single concept, a new method of physical, intellectual, and moral education. The success of Kano is to be linked to the in-depth changes that occurred in Japanese society, a country that within just a generation moved from a rural to an industrial economy. Chapter two is centered on jujutsu in the U.S. Cultural history usually makes a clear distinction between a rooting period and a diffusion period. Here, the rooting period sees the apparition of the Japanese method in the country, first in its jujutsu form. It starts at the end of the 19th century when Japan's culture and civilization began to be exhibited and admired overseas. Profoundly linked with immigration waves, the rooting period proceeded in different ways in Asian and Caucasian communities. Chapter three focuses on the shift from jujutsu to judo. It shows the leading role of Japanese Americans. But it also depicts the ethnic barriers restricting judo mostly to people of Asian ancestry. The dramatic events of World War II changed the face of judo in the U.S. As a direct consequence, the method of Kano had its cultural values reinforced and at the same time a nationwide diffusion started as the Japanese internees resettled.

In chapter four, postwar judo is presented as having reached a larger public. The sport orientation that U.S. judo leaders tried to promote was extremely influential. It was a strong motor of development. Throughout the country sports events started to be held, and competitions were a strong vector of the growth of judo in the 1950s and 1960s. The geographic diffusion was gradually reinforced by the impact of television and the press. Chapter five deals with contemporary judo in connection with the evolution of American society, the changing mores, and the growing interest of the nation in international records and medals.

This book finally deals with the "sportification" of a martial art. It studies the commitment of those who dedicated their lives to educational purposes following the precepts of Kano, transmitting their knowledge as a heritage to future generations. But, judo as a cultural object is also a sign of the needs and desires of the times and from that perspective, judo history reflects a constant adaptation to the evolution of American society.

Judo training at the Fumiji-cho dojo. Painting by Hishida Shunso (detail).

JUDO IN JAPAN

The history of judo in the United States starts with the understanding of its development in Japan. During a period of deep changes in Japanese society, a complex network of conflicting influences led to the evolution of martial arts techniques. The life and work of Kano Jigoro, the founder of Kodokan judo, played a pivotal role in the shift from jujutsu to judo in Japan. Devoted to the educational values of sports, he was instrumental in the initial promulgation of judo worldwide.

THE FIGHTING ARTS OF THE JAPANESE WARRIOR

The image of today's Japanese methods dates back to the beginning of the 20th century. Present-day disciplines, however, cannot be adequately understood without reference to the processes of development that have brought us to the point at which we stand today. While modern disciplines appear in 1868 with the modernization of Japan, the origins of the classical ones are rooted in history. Here some definitions are in order. Bujutsu (*bu, bushi,* warrior and *jutsu,* art) encompasses the *jutsu* forms, those combat systems whose names include the suffix *jutsu* as *kenjutsu,* sword art; *ninjutsu,* espionage; *chikujojutsu,* art of field fortification; *senjojutsu,* tactics; *jujutsu,* a generic term for a variety of systems of fighting while minimally armed, etc. (sumo being an exception).

Budo (*do,* "enlightenment," stage of training, way) uses the suffix *do* for identification purposes as in kendo, judo, karatedo, aikido. The jutsu forms were developed from the 10th century onward. They were meant for battlefield use. They constitute the classical disciplines.

The figure of the Japanese warrior dominates the evo-

Courtesy of the Kodokan Institute

lution of the classical martial arts. He has been known to play various parts and several functions in Japanese society. At times, he is presented as an admired ruffian. He can be a miserable henchman or a notorious general. He is the axis of the history of martial arts in Japan. The hazards of his influence and of his status explain the successive transformations of these practices.

From its earliest recorded history in the *Nihon Shoki*, the Chronicle of Japan, in 720 A.D., and for hundreds of years before, Japan was ruled by an emperor and his imperial court and family. The emperor was known to have been descended from the gods. This rule lasted for hundreds of years until the end of the Fujiwara Period and the beginning of the Kamakura Period (1185–1333). Then military leaders gained control and the country was ruled by a supreme commander known as the *shogun*, and his administration was known as the *bakufu*.

The 16th century is called the Warring Period (*Sengoku Jidai*) in Japan because no identified clan claimed the seat of the *shogun* and the clans continually fought each other to wrestle for that seat of power. Japan was in serious civil war for a hundred years. Toward the end of that century, three great leaders began the unification of the country through military power and conquests: Oda Nobunaga, Toyotomi Hideyoshi, and finally Tokugawa Ieyasu. Ieyasu was the one who wrestled final control of the country from all other clans, moving the capital of Japan from Kyoto to Tokyo and beginning two-and-a-half centuries of continued peace.

Until Ieyasu, fighting was a way of life for the samurai or *bushi*, and consequently the fighting arts held great importance. Warriors used bows and arrows for long distance attacks, and in close combat used swords and spears. When they lost their weapons, they had to use their bare hands. The fighting arts using bare hands were developed into systems of attack and defense and were known by a number of names such as *yawara*, *taijutsu*, *torite*, or *ku-miuchi*. Ultimately they came to be known as jujutsu, or literally, the techniques of *yawara* or gentleness.

Different clans and jujutsu masters developed different styles. One of the earliest and most prominent was known as the *Takenouchi Ryu*, which was founded in 1532. Other schools also developed, including *Kito Ryu*, *Tenshin Shinyo Ryu*, *Sekiguchi Ryu*, and the *Kyushin Ryu*. The main differences among the various schools of jujutsu had to do with particular styles and specialization of specific maneuvers by their founders.

Jujutsu

Bushido

Courtesy of the Kodokan Institute

The jujutsu that was practiced during the centuries of military rule in Japan until Ieyasu was a combination of techniques that, when applied, resulted in death or maiming. They were actually used in battles and one's prowess in the fighting arts meant life or death for oneself and survival or destruction of one's clan. They were brutal and real. The philosophy or way of the warrior during this period of Japanese history was one that centered on the importance of honorable death, as reported in the *Hagakure* by Yamamoto Tsunetomo.

Judo

THE MARTIAL WAYS OF JAPAN

When Ieyasu came to power in 1600, he moved the capital to Tokyo and established a system of rule over the country that finally brought peace and unity that lasted the entire Tokugawa Period of Japan, that is, until 1868. Among the many rules established by the Tokugawa shogunate was that the *daimyo*, leaders, from each of the clans needed to spend a substantial portion of their time in Tokyo with Ieyasu. They served essentially as political hostages so that clans would not attack Ieyasu or his allies so that peace could be maintained. Ieyasu also closed the country off from outside influence, banning foreigners and foreign products from coming into the country and Japanese from leaving the islands. The archipelago was essentially sealed off from the rest of the world for over 250 years.

The practice and meaning of martial arts and jujutsu evolved during the two-and-a-half centuries of Tokugawa rule. For the first few generations after Tokugawa took control of the country, warriors continued their practice of jujutsu with the full intent and understanding that their techniques might possibly be used in the battlefields once again. And during the first 50 years of Tokugawa rule, there indeed were a number of battles and rebellions that had to be dealt with, such as the capture of Osaka Castle in 1614–1615 and the Shimabara Rebellion in 1637–1638.

Courtesy of the Kodokan Institute

Zen

7

But as peace flourished, over time the practice and meaning of the fighting arts changed. People came to question the validity of the arts and their purpose in society. If there were no wars, why were people practicing how to fight and kill? Many of the techniques and practice methods of jujutsu themselves came to be stylized rather than practical, and practice for the purpose of style rather than for the purpose of being able to kill someone became more and more the norm.

During this transformation of the martial arts, martial artists themselves struggled to find meaning in their practice of the arts. Thus over time they came to add the study of literature, calligraphy, poetry, and other cultural arts to their repertoire. Of special importance were activities such as the practice of the tea ceremony, which actually had its first elevation in status by Toyotomi Hideyoshi's favored treatment of noted tea ceremonial master Sen no Rikyu. The year 1804, in fact, saw the beginning of the "Age of Culture." Warriors, therefore, were supposed to become not only accomplished in the ways of fighting and battle, but also learned scholars and cultural artisans in many respects.

In search of self-perfection, the individual elevated himself mentally and physically. Zen meditation taught the samurai to become self-reliant and self-denying. This spirit of abnegation has been instrumental in the constitution of the myth of the invincible warrior. In the moment of death, the warrior was to adopt a codified attitude that triggered the respect of others.

Dai Nihon Butoku Kai was established in April 1895 to revive *bushido* "for the purpose of patriotism and of raising the Japanese spirit." Ten years later, the *Butoku Kai* counted 1,037,791 members. About 60% of them belonged to kendo sections; judo had a "small" 20%.

In the 19th century, the Japanese public came to increasingly question the ways of the military leadership. After over 200 years of continued and lasting peace, people saw little benefit in the continued practice of the fighting arts. Over time the practice of jujutsu and other martial arts even came to be looked upon with disfavor. Martial artists and warriors in general, who were the only people allowed to wear their swords in public, contributed to these images of the warrior, as they engaged in challenge matches so as to seemingly protect their honor.

Discontent existed not only about warriors and the martial arts, but also about the military leadership as a whole. The Japanese public came to question many of the rules and laws that had been passed. In particular, the rights and privileges that were afforded to the warrior class, who were a step above others, were questioned, especially in times of continued peace when the need for such a class was no longer apparent.

Pressure built from outside Japan as well, from countries that wanted Japan to open its ports for trade and exchange. Yet, for over two centuries Japan had been closed off to the outside world and had refused any relationships with other countries. All of these social and political movements came to a head in 1853 when Commodore Perry brought his gunships into Tokyo Bay and demanded that he be able to dock his ships and open the country to others. While this was not what started the end of the Tokugawa Period, it was the straw that broke the camel's back because once the country was opened, it led to the realization that military law was no longer necessary or acceptable. These developments, along with the contributions of extraordinary individuals such as Saigo Takamori of Satsuma, Sakamoto Ryoma of Tosa, Ito Hirobumi of Choshu, and Katsu Kaishu from the *bakufu*, brought about a change in the leadership of Japan once again, usurping power from the Tokugawa family and restoring it to the emperor. Thus came the period of Japanese history known as the Meiji Period, which was marked by the restoration of power to the emperor (hence, the Meiji Restoration).

Among the many laws that were instituted during the Meiji Period (1868–1912) were those that eliminated the distinctions, rights, and privileges of the warrior class. For example, in 1871 the decree abolishing the wearing of swords was instituted and warriors were no longer able to adorn themselves with their weapons. Even though the weapon had never been used, it was still a symbol of a

Courtesy of the Kodokan Institute

Kano at 18.

One of the judo jackets used by Kano Shihan when he was practicing *Tenjin Shin Yo* jujutsu.

Courtesy of the Kodokan Institute

higher, privileged warrior class, and the warriors were stripped of it.

The first decades of the Meiji Period were a tumultuous time for martial artists, who essentially saw their entire way of life and being slip away from them. During the early years of the Meiji Period, many warriors took up fights in public to attempt to redeem themselves and their honor. Yet these fights only led to an increased disfavor among the public toward the warrior class and the martial artists in general. Martial arts, and the ways of the warriors, which had been held in such high esteem for centuries, became associated with the past. They gave way to diplomacy, politics, internationalization, and education. All of a sudden they fell from the top of society to occupy a lower rung on the social ladder.

At the same time, however, during the Meiji Restoration, the evolution of Japanese society in general, and of its educative system in particular, put the stress on values such as discipline and ethics. Thus Yamagata Arimoto, commander-in-chief of the armies of the government, established bushido as the common moral basis of the new army, having in view as he admitted, "to turn every single individual into a samurai." Courage and patriotism were highly valued. Practices borrowed from bujutsu and budo were meant to develop these qualities. In this context, when the slogan of the day was *fukoku kyohei*, "a rich country and a strong army," bujutsu or budo-related activities can be seen as ideological vectors.

Courtesy of Kiku Masamune

Sake Brewing Co., Ltd.

Courtesy of the Kodokan Institute

The outside gate of the Eishoji temple where the Kodokan was founded.

KANO JIGORO

It was during this tumultuous period of Japanese history that Kano Jigoro lived. The history of judo is the history of the shift from a martial art to a modern sport and can be understood within the social, historical, and political context of Japan. It is as much the story of Kano, who devoted himself to the education of the youth of his country, blending traditions and modernity, using individual prowess for collective benefits.

The beginnings of judo are closely related to Kano's life and personality. He was born in the year of the monkey, on October 28, 1860, in what was then the little village of Mikage (more precisely, Settsuko-ku, Ubaragun, Mikagemura, Hamahigashi, which is currently Kobe city, Nada East district, Mikage-cho). Kano's birthplace was well known for sake brewing, and members of the Kano family were wealthy sake brewers. Today the brand name of that same company, *Kiku Masamune,* is widely known.

Very early in Kano's rigorous education Western influences were added to Eastern traditions and teachings. One of his grandfathers was a well-known poet and a scholar of Chinese. During the 1860s Kano's father was a high-ranking government official. A born organizer with a strong sense of social responsibility, he contributed to the modernization of Japan along Western lines, opening Hyogo Harbor to foreign trade and inviting Western-style ships. Young Kano in whom the same qualities were to be found later in life was obviously influenced by his father's spirit of enterprise.

Courtesy of the Kodokan Institute

Kano's diary.

Courtesy of the Kodokan Institute

The Kano family.

Courtesy of the Kodokan Institute

In 1870, soon after the death of Kano's mother, his father decided to move to Tokyo. It was then a time of great cultural and social ferment in Japan from which Kano obviously benefited. In Tokyo, already brought up on Confucian classics, he was put into another Confucian school. At the same time he was sent for English lessons to Mitsukuri Shuhei, a renowned scholar who was to belong to a group of influential thinkers dedicated to educational reforms. In his early teens, Kano developed a strong taste for math and showed a particular affinity for languages. His language skills were developed to the point that, during his study of jujutsu his notes were written in English, probably to secure the confidentiality of his research at a time of intense rivalry among jujutsu schools. In his old age, he also kept his diaries in English.

As a boy Kano was frail but quick-tempered. Being extremely gifted, he studied with boys who were older and bigger and he soon understood the need to find a way to defend himself. At the age of 14 (15 according to Japanese tradition), he entered the Foreign Languages School, which was part of the *Kaisei Gakko*. There Kano was one of the first Japanese to play baseball, introduced one year before by two American teachers. He loved the spirit of the sport, a new concept in Meiji Japan, and certainly found some inspiration in it later on. In 1877, he entered Tokyo Teikoku (Imperial) University, currently Tokyo University. Many among the teachers and students he met there were to become leading figures in Meiji life. Because he had to deal with well-built young men coming from all over the country, he decided to learn more about the art that enabled the weak to overcome the strong. In Tokyo, it was then very hard to find anyone who knew how to teach the ancient art of jujutsu. The *Kobusho*, the school of martial arts, where samurai youths had been taught jujutsu in the old days, had disappeared with the Meiji Restoration movement. Besides, jujutsu had been a composite of different systems, and this fragmentation had also been detrimental to the "gentle art" as it was called.

Jujutsu exhibition at the Iso Masatomo dojo.

Courtesy of the Kodokan Institute

In 1877, Kano was eager to learn more about this ancient practice. After months of research, he finally managed to find a former *Kobusho* jujutsu master, Fukuda Hachinosuke. Hachinosuke became his first teacher, which was reluctantly accepted by his father who saw no future in this old tradition. Kano took over Fukuda's school when he died, in 1877. He kept on studying with Fukuda's teacher, Iso Masatomo, but his interest for the academic subjects he studied such as philosophy, political science, and economics never flagged.

In 1881, he began to study the jujutsu of the *Kito* school with another *Kobusho* teacher, Iikubo Tsunetoshi, who replaced Iso after his death. This time the stress was put on the spiritual side of judo. Iikubo, an expert at throws, gave less importance to *kata,* but the main *kata* originally performed with armor, *koshiki no kata,* was kept. It was one of Kano's favorites; he performed it before the emperor in 1929. The *Kito* school is also at the origin of the name judo. Kano deliberately chose it to underline the moral side of his system.

THE KODOKAN JUDO

The year 1882 was a landmark year for Kano. He was appointed lecturer in politics and economics at *Gakushuuin* (the then private school for the nobility) where he was to teach for some years and then served as a director. He also started a private school, the *Kano Juku,* and an English language school. *Kano Juku* was a preparatory school whose main goal was to build the character of the pupils who lived there. This year is said to be the date of the formal beginning of his judo

Kano met jujutsu masters at the *Dai Nihon Butoku Kai* in July 1906.

*Seiryoku
Zenyo.
"The best use
of energy"*
**Calligraphy
by Kano
Shihan.**

academy, the Kodokan, in a space rented from a small Buddhist monastery in Tokyo. The number of his students swelled rapidly; coming from all over Japan, many left old jujutsu masters to train with Kano. Kano's method was adopted by the police and the navy, introduced to schools and universities, and rapidly spread overseas. What came to be known as Kodokan judo was a synthesis of several schools of jujutsu to which he added ideas taken from interviews, readings, and forgotten techniques. In 1889, after his first foreign trip, during which he had inspected educational facilities in Europe, he got married and eventually had eight children.

Kano was a noted educator. He occupied several positions as headmaster of various schools and the Tokyo Teachers Training College. He was considered a most articulate spokesman in educational matters. Kano's genius essentially lies in the fact that he viewed judo as closely linked with education and adapted it accordingly. He saw and developed the guiding principle behind jujutsu where others had just seen a collection of techniques. The ultimate goal was to make the most efficient use of mental and physical energy. Each combination of movements represented a set of ideas. He rejected techniques that clashed with his conception of life. He paid attention to every single aspect of judo and to its potentialities. Judo etiquette, the aesthetic side of judo, was as much a part of this mental and physical discipline as the methods of defense and attack.

Even if judo is based on techniques derived from jujutsu, Kano's deep concerns were obvious when he wrote in December 1904 in the preface of the book by Sumitomo Arima, *Judo, Japanese Physical Culture:* "The prosperity of a country depends on the fullness of the nation's energy, which in turn is inseparably linked with the efficient training of people's mind and body. Hence all the powers of the World are busy trying every means to enhance their national strength. With this end in view they devote, *inter alia,* their unstinted efforts to physical culture, and there is no country but has some methods characteristically its own, with which it endeavors to foster the national vigor."

The principles of judo worked inside and outside the dojo, in the workplace, the school, the political world, everywhere. What is fascinating about Kano's life is that, apart from the exceptional qualities of the founder of judo, the forces that were to cause the international success of this discipline were already at work in the early days of his teachings. In 1919, in Tokyo, Kano met John Dewey, who was then a guest lecturer at the Imperial University.

*Jita Kyoei.
"Mutual
prosperity"*
**Calligraphy
by Kano
Shihan.**

They exchanged views on education. Various parallels could be drawn from their philosophical concepts. On a Sunday morning, Kano took Dewey to the Kodokan to show him how his ideas could be illustrated on a mat. Dewey was fascinated: "It is really an art." He admired the way the laws of mechanics were blended with old practices and added to Zen Buddhist teachings. The founder of the American educational system immediately saw the importance of Kano's teachings: "It is much better than most of our inside formal gymnastics. The mental element is much stronger." Kano's method derived from old-style ju-jutsu techniques but it definitely differed from the methods of the past. Getting rid of all dangerous, killing, or maiming jujutsu *waza* (technique), Kano forced opponents to grapple with one another. Thus he restricted violence. So as to make them safer he improved falling techniques. Whereas it had always been understood mainly as a goal, victory now became a means of building people's character. But this method differed mainly because it referred to science and rationalism. Turning his back to the traditional ways of teaching, Kano liked to explain judo techniques scientifically, studying attitudes, forces at play, problems of equilibrium, center of gravity moves. In 1895, throwing techniques were classified into five different sets (*go kyo no waza*).

In his study of Kano's life, David Waterhouse emphasizes the complexity and the diversity of his philosophy of education. He shows how Kano borrowed heavily from a long tradition of thought in which mostly Confucian and also Buddhist elements merged with Taoism and Shinto. A Neo-Confucian philosopher of the 16th century already claimed that "knowing" implied "doing." This heritage was common to Kano and his contemporaries who equally drew from contemporary national and Western studies on education. Kano Jigoro's strategy in the field of education was three-pronged: the acquisition of knowledge, the teaching of morality, and the training of one's body by physical education. The *san iku shugi*, or "principle of the three educations," was a popular theory at the time, certainly adapted from Herbert Spencer, one of the most discussed Victorian thinkers, and from others.

As an educator, Kano advocated the "three culture principle." He made this point clear when he wrote: "a healthy

1936 Olympic Games in Berlin. Kano Jigoro at the podium ceremony after the victory of Jesse Owens.

Kano accepts Pierre de Coubertin's invitation.

Courtesy of the Kodokan Institute

body is a condition not only necessary for existence but as a foundation for mental and spiritual activities." He insisted on the purpose of physical exercise: "No matter how healthy a person may be if he does not profit society his existence is vain." *Taiiku,* physical education, was an important factor of Kodokan judo. In the Kodokan magazines, *Kokushi* (1888–1903) and *Judo* (1915 to the present), articles about physical education were numerous. Kano saw the training of physical education instructors as essential. When Kano was in charge of the Teachers Training College he established a physical education department there, with a wide range of sports. Kano designed judo as a way to develop harmoniously the intellectual, moral, and physical aspects of the education of young people.

Kano repeatedly showed how the efficient use of one's mind and body was the key to self-fulfillment. But he added to this the Confucian concept of social obligation and consequently helping others to learn or teach was part of the process. Kano's principles were summed up in the two mottoes of the Kodokan Cultural Society founded in 1922: *Seiryoku Zenyo* and *Jita Kyoei,* that is, one must make good use of his spirit and physical strength for the common good and to reach self-realization.

In 1909, Japan received an invitation to take part in the International Olympic Committee from Baron Pierre de Coubertin, the father of the modern-day Olympics. Kano was chosen as Japan's representative. Thirteen years had passed since the first modern Olympic Games were held in Athens, Greece, in 1896. However, there was still no participation from an Asian country. Kano was the first Asian member of the IOC. At the time there was no general sports organization in Japan that could send athletes to the Olympics. Thus in 1911, the Japan Amateur Athletic Association was founded and Kano was installed as the first president. At this meeting, it was decided that Japan would participate in its first Olympics at the 1912 Games to be held in Stockholm, Sweden.

This served as the basis for the development of all varieties of sports in Japan. After that time Kano continued his work as an IOC member and for that purpose he traveled extensively within Japan and abroad. He turned all his energies into the organization of sports in Japan. In 1938, in Cairo, the International Olympic Committee

Courtesy of the Kodokan Institute

accepted Japan's proposal; Tokyo was to be the site of the 12th Olympic Games. However, on May 4, 1938, Kano died of pneumonia aboard the *S.S. Hikawa Maru* on his way home, his last port of landing being Seattle, Washington. He was 79 years old.

Modern budo has no military function although it stemmed from the jutsu forms developed prior to the mid-18th century. If Japanese are now unable to distinguish between these two very different kinds of classical disciplines, it is because changes were made to accommodate the new role of martial arts to serve the needs of the government as a means of discipline for citizens; and these changes were made by people who associated bujutsu and budo. Modern disciplines are best described today as methods of self-defense. Indeed in the strictest sense, none of these modern techniques has much to do with martial arts or even martial ways. Little is left of the warlike quality in these practices. In today's Japanese society, budo is the most popular because of the wide range of its purposes. Still, as Donn Draeger puts it in *The Martial Arts and Ways of Japan*, to the traditionalists and to those who regard classical bujutsu from the viewpoint of actual combat, the modern disciplines are "nothing but an ass in a tiger's skin." An adherent of the spiritually oriented classical bujutsu may view

Kano Jigoro painted by Kanayama Heizo.

the modern disciplines as a brash and colossal sham, a mere empty shell.

Kano, however, breathed new meaning into this shell. In creating judo, he created a system of intellectual, moral, and physical development. Kano modified and adapted the techniques of jujutsu, which had outlived its day in Japan. By focusing on the development of character and ways of life and being, Kano was able to catapult judo from a lower-class activity for heathens to a method of dealing with social problems and concerns. The success of the transformation of the fighting systems of jujutsu into the development of the intellectual and moral systems of judo in Japan can easily be seen by the staggering increases in the popularity of judo in its earliest years. This transformation brought about stunning results, not only in Japan but around the world.

The Barnum & Bailey Greatest Show on Earth, 1912.

THE JUJUTSU VOGUE

Courtesy of the Kodokan Institute

The rooting of judo in America reflects the spirit of the times. The transplantation of the Japanese art of fighting was made possible because of a combination of social, cultural, and political events that led to a jujutsu vogue in the first decades of the 20th century. The artistic and the military facets of the Country of the Rising Sun had a strong appeal for the American public. It presented a new culture and new models to a society in evolution while the nation was involved in an intricate world policy that changed the balance of the world.

Lafcadio Hearn (1850–1904) emigrated to the U.S. at 19. When he was 40, he left for Japan to write a travel book and stayed there. He married the daughter of a high-ranking samurai, Koizumi Setsuko. He adopted her family name and became a Japanese subject in 1895. When admiration for Japan waned, he was to be the country's best ambassador.

THE RAGE FOR JAPAN

Sadakichi Hartmann, who came to the U.S. as a boy in 1882, was half-Japanese half-German. A brilliant art critic, he was one of the first writers who succeeded in popularizing the peculiarities and beauties of Japan.

America's fascination started after Commodore Perry's expeditions forced Japan to enter into trade and diplomatic relations with the Western world in 1853 and 1854. The event was widely publicized. In 1860, Japan sent its first delegation to the United States. After two centuries of seclusion, the Meiji Restoration lifted the veil over old Japan. In 1879, during a world tour, ex-President Ulysses Grant met the emperor of Japan, a step hitherto unimaginable. During his stay in Tokyo, the U.S. president was introduced to Japanese traditions and to a martial arts exhibition. Fukuda Hachinosuke who staged this event declared to young Kano: "We have been asked to perform jujutsu for the American president. Master Iso and I will perform Tenshin Shinyo kata. I would like you and Godai Ryusaku to demonstrate randori." The demonstration was held on August 5. The president watched carefully. Afterward, Fukuda reportedly said to Kano: "Well done! That was a fine display. The president is very interested in jujutsu. He said he'd like to see jujutsu become popular in the United States."

USJF Archives

"The principles of the art may be defined briefly as the process of turning an enemy's exertion into one's advantage, in other words, jiu-jitsu avoids resistance with strength against strength, that is, a method of achieving ultimate victory by inviting an initial defeat."

Yae Kichi Yabe,
MacFadden Physical Development,
February 1905.

During the Meiji era, communications were made easier, contacts and cultural ties were established, friendships were formed. Self-supporting Japanese students chose to travel to America; many graduated from prestigious universities. Some of those who studied at Harvard Law School became part of the Japanese elite. American professors were invited to teach at Tokyo Imperial University; businessmen and travelers visited Japan. Imported works of Japanese art and Japanese pavilions at various World Fairs had a powerful impact on art lovers and mostly on impressionist painters. The influence of "Japanism" was strong. Artists in Europe and in the United States found new sources of inspiration in Japanese culture and aesthetics. The promotion of Asian arts by American scholars like Ernest Fenollosa, curator of the Imperial Museum in Tokyo, and Sadakichi Hartmann, art critic, helped Americans to better understand the Japanese artistic heritage.

The paintings of John Le Farge, Helen Hyde, Mary Cassatt, and James McNeill Whistler strengthened the growing interest in Japanese culture. Asian designs and motifs became popular. Japanese goods and artifacts including pieces of art, bone china, and literature appealed to many Americans. Lectures and articles praised the rare charm of Japanese life with its delightful old customs. Like Perry's narratives they triggered interest in an existence simpler and healthier than American life. They prompted more observers to make extended visits to Japan.

In 1891, Kano, who had just toured educational facilities in Europe, was given the position of principal of Kumamoto Government College. In this age concerned with the quest for new methods in education, the founder of judo recruited Lafcadio Hearn as a teacher. The celebrated journalist was so impressed with the method of Kano that he called "jiujutsu" that he dedicated a long essay to it. He analyzed the Japanese art of self-defense as an integral part of Japanese culture and deciphered its intricate implications. In a system in which defense, philosophy, economy, and morals cross-pollinated one another, he also foresaw the importance of the political context and how it might dwarf the potentialities of this art.

In *Out of the East,* Hearn eloquently presented an idealized view of the magic of judo: "What Western brain could have elaborated this strange teaching, never to oppose force by force, but only direct and utilize the power of attack; to overthrow the enemy solely through his own strength—to vanquish him solely by his own efforts?

Surely none! The Western mind appears to work in

Higashi Katsukuma from
The Complete Kano Jiu-Jitsu (Judo), **1905.**

Various styles were in use in the early 1900s. Kano's method had not yet reached its full development. Only some Japanese and American instructors had been taught at the Kodokan Institute. Others came from older schools and performed more traditional techniques. Besides, Kano's pupils had to prove their efficiency in real combat, narrowing again the distance between jujutsu and judo. For the general public, spotting the difference between styles was not really an issue in those days.

The Japanese ultimatum to Russia rendered by French cartoonist Caran d'Ache, 1905.

straight lines; the Oriental, in wonderful curves and circles. Yet how fine a symbolism of Intelligence as a means of foiling brute force! Much more than a science of defense is this jiujutsu: it is a philosophical system; it is an economical system; it is an ethical system (indeed, I may say that a very large part of jiujutsu training is purely moral); and it is, above all, the expression of a racial genius as yet but faintly perceived by these Powers who dream of further aggrandizement in the East." Hearn also drew a convincing parallel between the art of jujutsu and Japan's policy. In 1895, after the victory against China, he wrote: "Japan has won in her jiujutsu," meaning the Japanese had used the principle of yielding in order to conquer.

Positive representations of artistic and romantic Japan were soon counterbalanced. The turn of the 20th century saw Japan shoot to the forefront of international politics. Within just a few decades of its opening, Japan became the leading political and military powerhouse in all of Asia. Japan's diplomatic history entered a new phase. Struggling to gain leverage in newfound international politics, Japan concluded a trade treaty with China in 1871 and took control over the Ryukyu Islands, currently Okinawa, in 1872. In 1876, Japan opened Korea just as the U.S. had opened Japan 23 years prior, by sending warships. With these developments, Japan came to compete with Russia and China for influence in the Far East. In 1894, Japan started a phase of expansionism that was going to impair its relations with the United States. The absence of serious clashes of interests before this had made mutual understanding and cultural cooperation easier. However, its victory over China in 1895 alarmed the Europeans and the Americans. In 1900, the Japanese joined the international relief expeditions to Beijing at the time of the Boxer Rebellion. Fear of Russian expansion into China and Korea led to the Japanese attack on the Russians in 1904 at Port Arthur. The victory of Admiral Togo, who crushed the Russian fleet in the straits of Tsushima in May 1905, put an end to this war.

Book covers reflect images of military Japan and reveal the persisting blending of jujutsu and Kano's method.

21

USJF Archives

Jujutsu, an art and a science emblematic of the Country of the Rising Sun.

The year 1905 was crucial. It was above all the first time in the modern era in which an Asian power had defeated a European nation. As Japan entered the arena of world politics as a powerful rival, the background gradually became more complex and it most certainly influenced the destiny of judo. Better than a simple publicity gimmick, the image of the "small Yellow Man flooring the Russian ogre" proved to be clear evidence of the efficiency of jujutsu, in a context of strong American-Russian rivalry. In the feverish quest for answers after the Japanese feats, jujutsu was at the center of the military and political debate.

These historical events brought with them an unprecedented interest in the small island nation of Japan. European and American observers looked upon Japan with wonder and caution. Not knowing much about Japan previously, they searched for answers as to how an island nation, which had been closed off from outside influences for centuries, could come to exert such major influence in the Asian continent in such a short amount of time, bringing large countries such as China and Russia to their knees in war. Military leaders and educators who were bewildered by the feats of the Japanese soldier pointed out the union of mind and body. They looked upon Japanese preparedness as a unique combination of physical training—jujutsu—and code of honor—*bushido*.

Curiosity and interest contributed greatly to the publication of articles and books focusing on the warrior code. The most well-known work that propounded this view was that by Nitobe Inazo. In his 1905 *Bushido: The Soul of Japan*, Nitobe tried to explain the Japanese character using the concepts of the feudal warrior or samurai. The *bushido* that permeated the Japanese character was composed of a set of core values that included honor and justice, politeness and sincerity, loyalty and self-control. Stoicism was a major part of *bushido*, as were the two different types of obligations, *giri* and *on*. Physical training and education in the *bushido* way were based on the three major principles of wisdom, benevolence, and courage.

In March 1905, in Mukden, Manchuria, an important battle in the Russo-Japanese war took place. It was seen as the first great victory of the Japanese, and an astonishing revelation of Japanese strength. The efficiency of the Japanese army during hand-to-hand fights puzzled observers. A journalist underscored the fact that a physician had seen many wounded soldiers on the battlefront, with broken limbs or disarticulations. The amazing victory of Japan over Russia reinforced the myth of Nipponese invincibility. In Europe, some underscored the role played by jujutsu in the battle of Mukden: "*The triumph of Japan was to insure the popularity of jiu-jitsu [. . .] Today, in order to explain Japan's superiority, informed people assert: Jiu-jitsu won the battle of Mukden!*" During the same period, a renowned travel writer, Douglas Brooke Wheelton Sladen, noted: "*The wiry little Japanese have Jujitsu'd the three biggest men on the Russian flag-ship.*"

USJF Archives

In 1902, Samuel Hill invited Yamashita Yoshitsugu to teach his children judo. Formerly a lawyer, Samuel Hill worked for James J. Hill, the founder of the Great Northern Railroad, before he married one of his boss's daughters, Mary Frances, and became an enthusiastic and charismatic road builder. Gathering information on highways like the Trans-Siberian, Hill frequently traveled to Europe and Asia. He decided that judo, which he had seen demonstrated during a recent business trip to Japan, would be just the "thing to imbue young James Nathan Hill with the ideals of the Samurai class, for that class of men is a noble, high-minded class" according to Joseph Svinth's study about judo pioneers. In this age concerned about character development, judo was obviously viewed by Hill as the best solution to improve the health and behavior of his spoiled and puny nine-year-old son.

Courtesy of the Kodokan Institute

Yamashita was one of the so-called "four great pillars" of the Kodokan and Kano's right hand man. Actually, the judo expert did not stay long with Hill. He moved to the District of Columbia where he gave the Japanese Legation some lessons. Commander Takeshita Isamu, the Japanese naval attaché, arranged for Professor Yamashita to meet President Theodore Roosevelt in the White House. On March 5, 1904, Roosevelt wrote to his son: "Dear Kermit, I am wrestling with two Japanese wrestlers three times a week. I am not the age or the build one would think to be whirled lightly over an opponent's head and batted down on a mattress without damage. But they are so skillful that I have not been hurt at all. My throat is a little sore, because once when one of them had a strangle hold I also got hold of his windpipe and thought I could perhaps choke him off before he could choke me. However, he got ahead."

Actually, Roosevelt's interest in jujutsu was stirred earlier on by one of his relations, William Sturgis Bigelow. An admirer of samurai "sports" and an art collector, Bigelow was anxious to make Roosevelt a staunch partisan of Japan. He had discovered jujutsu in 1882 and trained with Okakura Kazuko, who became a key figure of American martial arts. In 1901, with the help of the unfortunate secretary of war whom Bigelow had

Mrs. Yamashita and Mrs. Wadsworth, a member of the Washington elite.

Courtesy of the Kodokan Institute

"White House, April 9, 1904, Dear Ted, I am very glad I have been doing this Japanese wrestling, but when I am through with it this time I am not at all sure I shall ever try it again while I am so busy with other work as I am now. Often by the time I get to five o'clock in the afternoon I will be feeling like a stewed owl, after an eight hours' grapple with Senators, Congressmen, etc.; then I find the wrestling a trifle too vehement for mere rest. My right ankle and my left wrist and one thumb and both great toes are swollen sufficiently to more or less impair their usefulness, and I am well mottled with bruises elsewhere. Still I have made good progress, and since you left they have taught me three new throws that are perfect corkers."

Theodore Roosevelt's Letters to His Children.

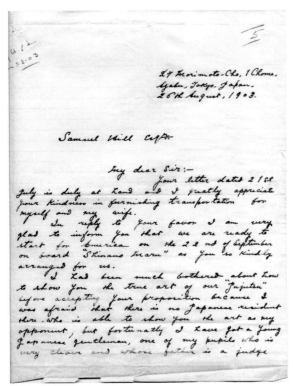

Courtesy of Mary Hill Museum of Art

pinned down on the floor, he demonstrated the efficiency of some holds of this Japanese style of wrestling to the president. In 1903, on his way back from Japan, Bigelow offered Roosevelt six judo jackets, a book about judo, and a supply of Japanese green tea. Then, he insisted the President should start practicing with John J. O'Brien, who had spent ten years in Nagasaki as police inspector and had been taught jujutsu. To better grasp original expertise, a Japanese authority on judo, Yamashita, was introduced to the White House soon after. There, President Roosevelt had prepared a separate room to take his lessons. This "judo room," the first White House dojo so to speak, stands out as a place where Roosevelt spent part of his legendary energy, and where he had a vicarious relation with Japan's might. All the while, he apparently liked to use jujutsu in letters and dinner conversations as a decisive argument to explain the subtleties of world events. Later Roosevelt secured a position for Yamashita at the U.S. Naval Academy. In *Getting a Grip, Judo in the Nikkei Communities of the Pacific Northwest 1900–1950*, Joseph R. Svinth mentions: "Training took place Monday, Wednesday, and Friday afternoons. He earned $1,666 for the semester, but had to pay his own assistants. The class had about 25 students." Yamashita and his wife also taught upper-class people in Washington, notably the wives and children of politicians and prominent individuals in society.

On August 26, 1903, Yamashita replied to Samuel Hill: "*My dear Sir, [. . .] In reply to your favor I am very glad to inform you that we are ready to start for America on the 22nd of September on board 'Shinano Maruë' as you so kindly arranged for us. I had been much bothered about how to show you the true art of our 'jujutsu' before accepting your proposition because I was afraid that there is no Japanese resident there who is able to show you the art as my opponent, but fortunately I have got a young Japanese gentleman, one of my pupils who is very clever and whose father is a judge of the Tokyo Supreme Court, who voluntarily applied to go to America with us at his own expense which I have gladly consented to. Asking you to give our kindest regards to Mrs. Samuel Hill and your son.*"

The Yamashitas and friends in front of the White House.

Courtesy of the Kodokan Institute

THE STRENUOUS LIFE MYSTIQUE
AND THE "JAPANESE ART"

The "Japanese art" was often linked with science and anatomy and was considered a sophisticated means of defending oneself. Actually, physical educators who in many cases had being associated with the upper-class system of education promoted physical practices in accordance with established manners and self-control. Thus, the appeal of the Japanese method besides its efficiency relied as much on a scientific knowledge of the human body as on social distinction. Theodore Roosevelt as zealous sportsman was emblematic of this movement. He had outgrown a sickly childhood by practicing daily exercise. At Harvard, he actively practiced boxing and wrestling, among other sports. Later he promoted a cult of masculinity through essays published before the Spanish American War. A strenuous life was meant to turn men into leaders who would contribute significantly to the common weal. Roosevelt's heroism there invited voguish press coverage and stood for a model of sport's efficiency in molding a man for an active and creative life. His expertise in riding and marksmanship caught the imagination of his fellow Americans, in all walks of life. He became uncommonly popular with mass America. He exemplified post-1890 U.S. foreign policy: the use of force to maintain order. For Roosevelt sport and politics were intertwined.

His interest in judo can certainly be explained by his circle of Japan-oriented New England friends, his faith in boundless energy, the athletic qualities required, but also the magic elements the combat tricks implied. The strenuous life mystique was in a way reflected in the ideology of the period. Roosevelt had the tendency to cast every issue in moral and patriotic terms. He believed the American future rested on events in Asia. Keeping Asian

Courtesy of Todd-MacLean Physical Culture Collection, The University of Texas at Austin

MacFadden's magazine, *Physical Culture*, featuring President Roosevelt, September 1904.

USJF Archives

markets was essential. Siding with Japan after the 1904 Japanese surprise attack was strategic, and learning the potential rival's judo tricks was probably part of his special brand of diplomacy.

However, outstanding individuals were not the only ones to generate the passion for sport. Physical exercise and sport were recognized for the rough and strenuous experience they could provide and they were promoted because of their impact on individual mentality and social behavior. Whether real or excessive, the reputation of jujutsu's efficiency remained its most remarkable characteristic and was to be the dynamo of its development. Military schools and police academies of numerous countries were to experiment with this new practice. Envoys were sent to Japan to learn about that method while emissaries from Japan were brought in. From 1900 onward, jujutsu was definitely a Japanese "export" in the United States as well as in most European countries like France, Germany, Great Britain, Sweden, Austria, Holland, Italy, Spain, and Portugal.

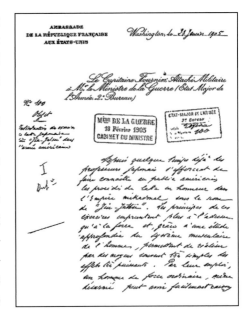

January 28, 1905, Captain Fournier, intelligence officer of the French Ministry of War, reports from Washington on "*Jiu-jitsu in the U.S. Army.*"

USJF Archives

Fort Myer, Virginia, 1918.

COUNTRY	YEAR	INSTRUCTOR	INSTITUTION
USA	1905	Yamashita	Naval Academy
FRANCE	1905	Ré-Nié	Paris Police
GREAT BRITIAN	1905	Tani	Admirality (Portsmouth)
GERMANY	1906	Ono	Berlin Military School

Courtesy of the Kodokan Institute

Maeda (seated center) in Boston, 1905.

A year after Yamashita, Tomita Tsunejiro assisted by Maeda Mitsuyo arrived in the U.S. to teach judo. Tomita was the first person to officially sign the Kodokan roll books. In *A Lion's Dream*, Kouyama Norio remembers the short stay of Maeda, whose action was decisive in the introduction of judo into Brazil some years later. He recalls a demonstration at West Point where neither Maeda, who was not familiar with Greco-Roman wrestling rules, nor Tomita, who was beaten by a much stronger opponent could convince the cadets of their efficiency. The two men parted. Tomita went to the West Coast. Maeda stayed in New York for a while teaching judo at Princeton University. According to Kouyama, Maeda was approached to engage in a match for prize money with a Brooklyn wrestler nicknamed "Butcherboy." Maeda won the match that took place in the Catskills. This was the beginning of the long career as a professional fighter Maeda followed in Brazil under the nickname of "Conde Koma."

These accounts, a few among many, are a good reflection of the impact of the Japanese method as it was at the beginnings of the 20th century. They throw into relief different elements. First, the fascination for Japanese culture and the victories of the Nipponese armies facilitated the introduction of jujutsu in America. Second, these stories highlight the interest shown by high-status people for a physical activity mixing elegance and efficiency, scientific knowledge and cultural patrimony, in other words traditions and modernity.

However, to these factors must be added the consequences of the urbanization process and the huge increase in population, which had a crucial impact in the field of sport. It resulted in new social needs and offers, and triggered changes in ways of life, as sport practice, especially team sports, played a growing role in American culture. The scope of immigration movement was a leading factor. Actually jujutsu and judo benefited largely from some of these developments, but in reaction also suffered restriction and even exclusion.

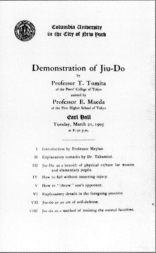

Courtesy of the Kodokan Institute

Courtesy of the Kodokan Institute

JUJUTSU FEVER

The image of Japan and especially its mystique came to play a central role in people's perceptions of Japanese culture and in particular martial arts. In a world transformed by industrialism and urban expansion, more and more leisure opportunities were offered to people. The Japanese Pavilion was one of the greatest successes of Philadelphia's Centennial Exhibition in 1876. Japanese art and culture were prominently displayed at the 1904 Louisiana Purchase Exposition during the World's Fair in Saint Louis, Missouri; the exhibition on Japan alone covered nearly seven acres. The Lewis and Clark Exposition in Portland, Oregon, in 1905 included a demonstration of Kitoryu jujutsu, one of the jujutsu styles studied by Kano Jigoro. The Japanese art of self-defense became introduced in cultural or entertaining events on both sides of the country.

Courtesy of the Kodokan Institute

Miss Dazie performing the "*Jiu-Jitsu dance*," New York, Ziegfeld Follies, 1907.

Young women and girls at Yamashita's dojo.

Music halls, dancing places, and vaudeville theaters attracted crowds, turning popular culture into a lucrative national product. At the same time, U.S. citizens understood sport as a mass spectacle, one of the many opportunities available in a society that glorified consumption. The combination of these factors led to a competition between managers eager to attract more spectators with innovative shows. Jujutsu bouts and the prowess of fighters supported by the fame of their armies and the mystique of the Orient immediately found its place. The jujutsu fever peaked in New York in 1907, the year of the first revue produced by Florenz Ziegfeld, the "Follies of 1907," when Daisy Peterkin, a.k.a. "Miss Dazie," performed the

Jerome Robbins Dance Division, The New York Public Library
for the Performing Arts, Astor, Lenox and Tilden Foundations

Courtesy of the Kodokan Institute

"jiu-jitsu dance" on the stage. The fact it was included in this show partly modeled on the Folies Bergère of Paris attests it entered the entertainment world as an object of fashion and an instrument of display. The Barnum & Bailey circus, a popular and gigantic spectacle, had its jujutsu fighters. For a 1912 show, the artists of the prestigious Strobridge Lithographic Company recreated the atmosphere of the circus on a poster featuring an "*Attraction Extraordinary: A Congress of Japan's Famous Strong Men, Gladiators, Swordsmen, Wrestlers, Jiu-Jitsu and Athletic Champions.*" Smaller shows like the Pantages also had their Japanese jujutsu troupe. In those days jujutsu was clearly displayed as an exotic practice. It was part and parcel of the culture of sensationalism.

Jujustu had become trendy to the point that even young film stars felt they had to show off their knowledge of it in the media. On March 19, 1916, a journalist of the *New York Telegraph* reported his interview with famous silent actress, Mary Miles Minter: "Miss Minter is, for a wonder, just the age that the publicity man claims, which is not quite fourteen, and she makes no attempt to appear anything else. One might think her a little older, because the experience of being a motion picture star has broadened her and given her an assurance that less talented girls have not had the opportunity of acquiring, yet she is above all simple and unassuming [...] She pointed through the window at a snowy street that sloped down toward the Hudson. 'This winter I've done lots of coasting on that hill, and I'm strong enough to take the boys' sleds away from them, which is lots of fun, because it makes them so angry. You don't know how strong I am. You see, I'm crazy about jiujitsu and have been taking lessons in it for some time. Also I like to box, because then I have an excuse to wave my arms about as much as I want to.' Miss Minter looked threateningly at the interviewer, but finally decided not to fracture the laws of hospitality."

In many places where prizefighting was not only common but symbolized the triumph of manly skills, the Japanese were engaged in numerous bouts. Wrestlers or even boxers kept challenging jujutsu specialists, and jujutsu remained part of the game. When the legendary Frank Gotch easily defeated Demetral the Greek, on March 11, 1916, *The Los Angeles Times* thus commented on the jujutsu bout

Courtesy of the Kodokan Institute

Tomita at the New York Heights Club. One of the six sections of the class in judo. "Fifty-five men trained on Monday night."

Momoe Japanese troupe, The Pantages, 1920–21 season.

USJF Archives

included in the program of the exhibition: "The boys who raised the racquet were four Japanese who threw each other over their shoulders, hips, heads and backs with wild abandon. At times it sounded as if the floor must give in from the force of the throw, but each time the fallen Jap came up smiling."

Many authors included the Japanese method in their treatises of combat sports or physical education. Notwithstanding, this open-minded attitude was not adopted by all. Professional wrestlers even used racial arguments to protect their cultural and commercial values. As in Paris and in Europe, they saw "the Yellow Man as an intruder in a Greco-Latin world up to now preserved." In Bernarr MacFadden's *Physical Development* magazine, Hugh Leonard, the wrestling instructor of the New York Athletic Club, declared in March 1905: "Our modern wrestling is a development of the sport as it was then known; but it has been so improved on and its possibilities have been so elaborated, that I think that as it is now, it is as perfect in a scientific way as it possibly can be. Now remembering the love of athletic exercises common to the leading white races, I do not believe that the 'little brown men,' in spite of their acknowledged ingenuity, can have evolved an art of attack and defense by unarmed man that is superior to our wrestling."

Such reactions demonstrate the limits of the popularity of the Japanese method. Restricted to upper-class people, to the Army and the Navy, jujutsu and judo were not considered a sport but an efficient, sophisticated, and typically cultural means of self-defense. President Roosevelt's opinion of the Japanese art of-

LEARN JIU-JITSU

THE JAPANESE NATIONAL SYSTEM OF PHYSICAL TRAINING AND SELF-DEFENSE

After being jealously guarded as a national secret for over two thousand years, a full exposition of the art of Jiu-Jitsu—the most wonderful and mysterious physical science in the whole world—will be given to the American public. Jiu-Jitsu embraces a system of physical training, which, without artificial means, develops every muscle and tissue and strengthens every organ in the human body. The Japanese, though small of stature, possess the most perfect physical development of any nationality, and attribute their wonderful strength and power of endurance solely to the practice of Jiu-Jitsu. As a means of self-defense Jiu-Jitsu is as potent at short range as the most deadly weapon. A knowledge of its self-preserving principles makes the timid man bold, courageous and self-reliant. There are over three hundred methods of weaponless warfare known to the art, any one of which will enable a man of average strength to dispose of the most formidable antagonist with an ease and rapidity which is astonishing. When once a person skilled in the art effects one of the Jiu-Jitsu "holds" it is utterly useless for an opponent to offer resistance. It makes no difference how unequally matched in point of size or strength the contestants may be, a knowledge of Jiu-Jitsu will enable a child of fourteen years to overcome and render powerless a man of thrice his strength.

FIRST LESSON SENT FREE

Mr. Y. K. Yabe, who has been the most successful teacher of the art in all Japan, has been delegated to give instruction in Jiu-Jitsu to Americans by correspondence. He has just written an intensely interesting book which explains the principles of this wonderful system and describes the evolution of Jiu-Jitsu during the past two thousand years. So long as the edition lasts, this book together with the first lesson in the art will be sent free to interested persons. The lesson is fully illustrated with full-page half-tone engravings, and teaches one of the most effective methods known to Jiu-Jitsu for disposing of a dangerous antagonist. If you want to learn all the closely guarded secrets of this marvelous science which for centuries past have been locked in the breasts of the *Samurai* ; if you would know how to defend yourself against any form of vicious attack and render helpless your assailant, you should write for this free book and specimen lesson today. It will be sent postpaid by return mail. Address
THE YABE SCHOOL OF JIU-JITSU, 351 A Realty Bldg., ROCHESTER, N.Y.

THE "VITAL TOUCH" ONE OF THE 300 EFFECTIVE METHODS KNOWN TO JIU JITSU FOR DISPOSING OF A DANGEROUS ANTAGONIST.

LARGEST WEEKLY CIRCULATION IN AMERICA

TIP TOP WEEKLY

AN IDEAL PUBLICATION FOR THE AMERICAN YOUTH

No. 482.   Price, Five Cents.

DICK MERRIWELL IN JAPAN

JUDO ART AGAINST JIU-JITSU

BY BURT L. STANDISH

"Augustly pardon, beneficent sir," murmured Brochan, smilingly, as he again fell on his back and, in that mysterious manner, sent Dick flying over his head to land flat on the ground.

Tip Top Weekly, July 8, 1905, "Dick Merriwell in Japan, Judo Art Against Jiu-Jitsu."

Frank Merriwell was the epitome of a sports hero. He was a Yale student, a self-made muscular Christian with great athletic skills. He exemplified traditional values such as hard work, courage, loyalty, and self-sacrifice. Because of the success of his novels, Burt L. Standish created a new character, Dick, Frank's young brother.

fers an interesting and relevant analysis of the problems linked to the rooting of judo in American sporting life as it was. As early as February 24, 1905, he wrote to his son: "Darling Kermit, [. . .] Since Sunday we have not been able to ride. I still box with Grant, who has now become the champion middleweight wrestler of the United States. Yesterday afternoon we had Professor Yamashita up here to wrestle with Grant. It was very interesting, but of course jiu-jitsu and our wrestling are so far apart that it is difficult to make any comparison between them. Wrestling is simply a sport with rules almost as conventional as those of tennis, while jiu-jitsu is really meant for practice in killing or disabling our adversary. In consequence, Grant did not know what to do except to put Yamashita on his back, and Yamashita was perfectly content to be on his back. Inside of a minute Yamashita had choked Grant, and inside of two minutes more he got an elbow hold on him that would have enabled him to break his arm; so that there is no question but that he could have put Grant out. So far this made it evident that the jiu-jitsu man could handle the ordinary wrestler. But Grant, in the actual wrestling and throwing was about as good as the Japanese, and he was so much stronger that he evidently hurt and wore out the Japanese. With a little practice in the art I am sure that one of our big wrestlers or boxers, simply because of his greatly superior strength, would be able to kill any of those Japanese, who though very good men for their inches and pounds are altogether too small to hold their own against big, powerful, quick men who are as well trained."

Roosevelt was not the only one to underline the superiority of brawn. The sensational reports of the new popular press and cheap pulp magazines that were widely read regularly echoed the exploits of strong men. They

USJF Archives

Tip Top Weekly, March 16, 1907, "The largest weekly circulation" pulp magazine.

The stories of the Merriwell brothers stimulated character development among young American boys.

USJF Archives

USJF Archives

Advertisement for John J. O'Brien's jujutsu course. O'Brien was the first instructor of President Theodore Roosevelt.

Bout between Seishiro
Okazaki and John
Morris, Hilo, Hawaii,
1925. According to oral
history, John Morris, a
heavyweight Ameri-
can boxing champion,
visited the islands
and challenged local
champions. He
defeated several
opponents causing
Japanese to lose face.
Then Okazaki
challenged Morris
and won the match.
Okazaki is said to have
received a gold watch
from the Japanese
community for
restoring its honor.

kept vivid the fame of jujutsu among Americans. How-ever, military Japan started to touch off scathing reviews, and defiant attitudes emerged after the war against Russia. Experts had first gained popular recognition by putting the stress on utility. They confined their art to the fields of the military, prizefighting, and self-defense courses. The glitter-ing exoticism that attracted crowds played a similar role imprisoning jujutsu and judo in a cultural enclave.

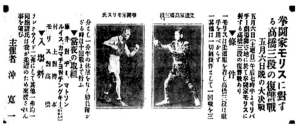

Courtesy of Georges Arrington, http://www.danzan.com

LIFE IN EARLY JAPANESE COMMUNITIES

While images of jujutsu, judo, and Japan itself were taking hold in the U.S. and around the world at the turn of the 20th century, the last stage of the rooting of judo in America was made possible by a wave of Japanese immigration. It gave a boost to the practice and allowed a decisive shift from jujutsu to Ka-no's method. At the same time it strengthened the cultural bonds of settlers' communities. Japanese emigration had three major causes. First, a sudden rise in land taxes was launched by the Japanese government in 1873 to support its activities toward modernization and westernization,

Courtesy of the JA Centennial Committee

"1923, devastating Tokyo earthquake fundraising drive. Ladies of Buddhist and Christian churches joined together in bun-dling food and clothing to send to refugees. Money was collected on street corners by Japanese mothers and daughters dressed in kimono from the larger Salt Lake population."

Japanese Americans in Utah.

Takagaki Shinz helped raise money by participating in a prize match on such an occasion.

Courtesy of the JA Centennial
Committee

resulting in a dispropor-
tionately heavy burden
on farmers. This was com-
pounded by the fact that
government spending in
relation to the Sino-Japa-
nese and Russo-Japanese
wars, and the trade imbal-
ance between Japan and
other countries, produced
high inflation, which fur-
ther reduced farmers' incomes. As a result, approximately
367,000 farmers lost their lands between 1883 and 1890.

Second, according to the conscription law young men
had to serve in the military. But, if they were able to stay
out of the country until they were 32 years old, they could
avoid serving. In addition, if the oldest male was abroad,
the second oldest male would then become the head
of the family, and in those cases the second oldest male
would not have to serve in the military. Finally, after the beginning of the Meiji Period, the Japanese government received numerous requests to send workers. These requests
came not only from the U.S., but also from countries such
as Australia, Canada, the West Indies, and what was then

JAPANESE IMMIGRANT AND JAPANESE AMERICAN POPULATION STATISTICS						
YEAR	TOTAL	NORTHEAST	MIDWEST	SOUTH	WEST	HAWAII
1900	85,437	535 (0.6%)	349 (0.4%)	66 (0.07%)	23,376 (27.4%)	61,111 (71.5%)
1910	151,832	1,915 (1.3%)	1,482 (0.9%)	610 (0.4%)	68,150 (44.9%)	79,675 (52.5%)
1930	278,465	4,014 (1.4%)	2,025 (0.7%)	1,126 (0.4%)	131,669 (47.3%)	139,631 (50.1%)
1950	325,976	7,438 (2.3%)	18,734 (5.7%)	3,055 (0.9%)	112,541 (34.5%)	184,611 (56.6%)
1970	588,324	39,125 (6.7%)	42,670 (7.3%)	28,504 (4.8%)	260,850 (44.3%)	217,175 (36.9%)
1990	847,562	74,202 (8.8%)	63,210 (7.5%)	67,193 (7.9%)	395,471 (46.7%)	247,486 (29.2%)

Source: U.S. Census, 1900–1990

the territory of Hawaii, annexed in 1898. Until 1885, Japan
had rejected these requests. Partially in response to the
problems many farmers had faced, the Japanese government became actively involved in sponsoring contract
laborers.

These three forces combined to urge many individuals,
mostly farmers, to find alternative ways to make a living. Some left agriculture to work in the silk industry;
others worked in mines and factories. One of the major
consequences was the emergence of the *dekasegi* philosophy—traveling to live temporarily in distant places in
order to make money to bring back or send home.

For example, Japanese migrants who went to Hawaii had
their passages paid plus $9 a month. They were provided

Courtesy of the
Kodokan Institute

Judo in Los
Angeles *circa* 1918
with Yamauchi
Toshitaka, Hirai
Yoshitaro, and Ito
Tokugoro.

with food, lodging, and medical care. The wage increase, coupled with the yen–dollar ratio, meant that a plantation laborer in Hawaii could earn six times more than a day laborer in Japan. They could save 400 yen, the amount that a silk worker could save by working every day and saving all wages for 10 years. Thus three years of contract labor seemed small compared to the anticipated income.

Despite the fact that the Chinese were barred from entering the U.S. after 1882, with the Chinese Exclusion Act, laborers were still needed in Hawaii and the West Coast. Hawaii, in particular, offered a chance to succeed because it struck a deal with the Japanese government to offer contract labor positions to Japanese immigrants from 1885 to 1894. In 1885, the Japanese government publicized the fact that it would offer 600 individuals the chance to go to Hawaii as contract laborers. They received 28,000 applications. The main impetus for these waves of immigrants was economic. In the U.S., the surge of newcomers who suffered heavy discrimination and hatred soured American relations. In 1907, the Roosevelt administration negotiated the "Gentlemen's Agreement" to calm California after several anti-Asian riots and to placate Tokyo officials. It was meant to check the immigration of laborers. But, the flow persisted especially after the Tokyo earthquake and so did racist attitudes. In 1924, with the National Origins Act the U.S. Congress virtually excluded Asian immigration. Friendships were severely shaken. Still, non-immigrant Japa-nese entered the U.S. as self-supporting students, temporary visitors, or businessmen.

Issei: the first-generation Japanese Americans. Issei are the parents of the Nisei and the grandparents of the Sansei.

YMBA athletic department. San Francisco, 1914.

Courtesy of the Buddhist Churches of America

Work in the early days of Japanese immigration was hard for both men and women. Men labored in plantations, fields, mills, or factories for most hours of the day, while women took up cleaning, cooking, and laundry services not only for their families but for their communities. To circumvent

Courtesy of Harold Yamada

the Alien land laws, the Japanese either placed the property in the names of their Nisei offspring, who were American citizens, or formed co-ops and then placed the co-op in the names of their children. As the Japanese communities grew, organizations were formed in order to safeguard their interests, like the Japanese Association of America, meant to promote the welfare of the Japanese immigrant population. Japanese interests and participation in both Buddhist and Christian churches played a major role in the lives of the immigrants. Clubs such as the Seinenkai, Young Person's Group, and the Educational Society known as the Gakuen cemented the immigrant communities and provided platforms for shared emotional support.

As the Japanese communities continued to assimilate into American culture and society, the generation gap between the Issei and Nisei was increased by a cultural gap. In general the Issei were quite identified with Japan. They spoke only Japanese, resisting learning English, and incorporated their old ways and traditions into their communities, press, and churches. The American-born Nisei were different. They knew that, in order to succeed in the U.S., they would have to absorb American culture. They inherited from their parents a remarkable desire to succeed in the face of hardship, but at the same time they learned the American definition of success. Once immersed in school, English was their primary language, and Japanese was reserved for use with families or friends. The standards accepted by the Issei parents were not satisfactory to many Nisei. There was thus a wide chasm between first- and second-generation Japanese. The Japanese American Citizens League, a civil rights organization that regularly highlighted assimilation and Americanization, was a good illustration of this gap. In fact, it sought to minimize cultural ties with Japan and focused its activities on the promotion of issues that would further encourage the assimilation and acculturation of the Nisei into American society.

Nisei: second-generation immigrant Japanese Americans. A distinction is made among the Nisei educated in the United States and the Kibei sent back as children to be educated in Japan.

The White River Dojo in 1927.

The White River Buddhist Church was opened in 1912. It was the leading cultural center of the valley. A Japanese language school was created in 1913.

Courtesy of the JA Centennial Committee

"1915. Ogden Buddhist sumo team. The team consisted of men who had just arrived in America from Japan."

Japanese Americans in Utah.

While the Issei recognized the fact that their Nisei children had to adopt American ways to succeed in the land, at the same time they put considerable pressure on them. For this reason many Nisei primary school children went to Japanese language school after their regular American school ended every day. When they got older, in middle school, they still went to Japanese language school once a week on the weekends.

Studies of cultural values, not only in the Japanese American communities but in other ethnic immigrant communities such as Koreans and Filipinos, indicate a trend that is relevant to the understanding of the development of judo. Contrary to what one would expect, studies have shown that Japanese Americans typically hold more conservative, more traditional, and more idealistic Japanese ideologies than Japanese in Japan or mainstream Americans do. In other words, they are more Japanese than native Japanese. This has occurred because of the way cultural values crystallized within immigrant communities. The Japanese culture that the Japanese immigrants and Japanese Americans knew was the Japanese culture that the first immigrants brought with them when they came to the U.S. between 1880 and the 1920s. That culture was that of Meiji Japan. As time passed and they assimilated into American society, the preservation of Japanese culture and customs centered around the preservation of this cultural system, which was the only one they knew. This explains why the Japanese culture that was developed over time was a particularly conservative and traditional one, even more so than that in Japan, because Japanese culture was actually changing in Japan as time progressed. For the Japanese American communities, a large part of the Japanese culture that they knew was that brought by their fathers and mothers before them. That type of Japanese culture has been preserved rigidly over time.

A Cultural Export

The crystallization of old Japanese culture stood in stark contrast to the American culture in which they lived. That is why there was a growing tension among the Japanese immigrant communities, one that contrasted the tradition and heritage of their original Japanese culture with the modernity and necessity of their new home's American culture. This tension and rift actually got larger with the Nisei children going to American schools, making American friends, speaking English, and adopting American ways and values. Fortunately sports and athletics were perfect outlets for this growing tension in the communities. Within this setting, social and cultural activities came to play a large role in the Japanese communities. Events like *obon*, the annual summer festival honoring one's ancestors, *oshogatsu*, the festivals welcoming the New Year, annual picnics, and other such activities kept the communities close together.

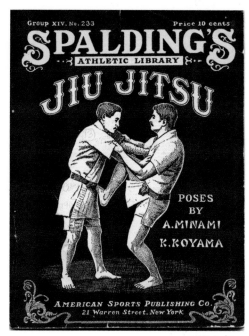

USJF Archives

Jiu Jitsu,
The effective
Japanese Mode
of Self-Defense,
American Sports
Publishing Co.,
1910.

Churches played a major role in the Japanese immigrant and Japanese American communities in the early years, and they still do today. Most of the Issei, and then most of their Nisei children, came from Buddhist backgrounds, and the Buddhist Church of America celebrates a long history in the U.S., having a major role in the social fabric of the lives of the immigrant Japanese communities. Buddhist priests and monks had traveled individually throughout the U.S. both from China and Japan for centuries. The Young Men's Buddhist churches had a key role in the lives of the Japanese communities. The church was not only a

Pre-World War I
postcard.

USJF Archives

Issei
practicing
in Hawaii
in 1902.

Courtesy of the Kodokan Institute

point of spiritual inspiration. Its many activities included Japanese language schools, English language training for the immigrants, a women's club, and many sport and athletic activities, including basketball, kendo, and judo. Because of a *de facto* segregation, especially in California, the Japanese were not encouraged to participate in public social events such as dances and parties. Thus, Nisei children began to organize their own social and athletic programs. Classes of *ikebana, chanoyu, noh, haiku, naginata*, Japanese cooking, kendo, karatedo, and judo were held in temples and churches.

On the mainland U.S., Seattle was the closest harbor, so the area developed a strong Japanese community. Svinth brings up a full-page description of the Seattle dojo in *The Seattle Times*, March 10, 1907. The Seattle dojo "was apparently organized sometime in late 1906, most likely by Kono [or Kano] Iitaro, a Kodokan 2-dan who had arrived in Seattle on May 20, 1903." This dojo is still operating today. Some months after Kono departed, another Japanese, Ito Tokugoro, replaced him as head instructor. Being involved in numerous challenges, Ito did a lot for the popularity of the Seattle dojo. The geographic spreading of judo on the West Coast can be traced on a map from large cities to smaller ones. Shortly thereafter the Tacoma dojo opened. In the 1920s, the Seattle and Tacoma dojos were the two main dojos in the state of Washington. Around 1930, some members of the Seattle dojo formed the Tentokukan Dojo. Smaller dojos, supported by larger ones, were founded in neighboring areas. Soon other dojos appeared all over the Northwest area, including Spokane, Yakima Valley, Eatonville, and in Oregon and Idaho. The same process is to be seen in Vancouver, British Columbia, Canada.

Kawaishi was born in 1899 in Himeji, near Kyoto, a piace from which many immigrants left. He was the sixth child out of seven. After college he graduated from the renowned Waseda University. He decided to depart for California after the 1923 Tokyo earthquake. He was then a Kodokan 4th dan, a high grade at that age in those days.

Studying part-time at San Diego University, he taught kendo and judo. He was also familiar with prizefighting. Then he went to New York and after a short stay in Brazil, he reached London in 1931 and finally settled down in Paris in 1935.

There, he established a westernized system that spread all over the world fitting non-Japanese players' expectations and becoming a professional business.

Kawaishi was most influential in the history of judo in the world. His almost 10-year-long stay in the United States was a formative period in the shaping of his views about judo for the West.

He can be credited with a leading role in the westernization process, that is, the adaptation of the Japanese method to Western mentalities and usages that started from Europe and led to today's judo.

The larger dojos in the Seattle area often recruited instructors from Japan. Many of these engaged in professional wrestling, not only to promote judo but also to help make a living. Ito, for example, held challenge matches for several years before traveling to South America. Judo started in the Los Angeles area when Ito returned there in 1915 and established the Rafu Dojo, which was kept open after his return to Japan. From 1915 to 1928 seven more dojos opened. But dojos also sprung up in the San Diego area, which was another port of entry for Japanese immigrants. Among the first instructors was Kawaishi Mikinosuke, who taught judo and kendo classes before leaving for New York City in 1927.

Hawaii was seemingly the cradle of judo in North America, and Kodokan archives show evidence that regular practice started on the islands as early as 1902. The first two Hawaiian judo clubs still exist today. The Shunyokan, a name given by Kano in 1913, was founded earlier on in 1909 by Teshima Shigemi and Kaneshige Naomatsu. Teshima enjoyed a close relationship with Kano Jigoro.

Thereafter, the Shobukan Judo Club was founded, and it still exists today on Kunawai Street in the Liliha area of Honolulu. In fact one of its original charter members, Migita Sunao, was still practicing until his recent passing in 1996. After that the Hawaii Chugakko (Junior High School) Judo Club was also founded, and for several years, the Shunyo Kan, Shobu Kan, and Chugakko judo clubs were the three largest clubs in the islands.

Celebration party of the opening of the New York Judo Club in 1929. (Kawaishi is seated in the middle center.)

Courtesy of the Kodokan Institute

Shobu Kan
judo club,
circa 1910.

USJF Archives

Among other pieces of evidence, the interviews conducted by Dr. John Masuhara in the 1970s can back up this statement showing that it was jujutsu and not Kodokan judo techniques that were most of the time taught in Hawaii and in Japanese communities in general prior to the 1920s. Thus, Sakamoto Sadao recalled his first instructor, Tanaka Kichimatsu, who had organized the Yoshin-Ryu dojo in 1912. "Tanaka Kichimatsu, as an employee of the old Yoshimura Store on Ferneaux Lane in Hilo Town, apprehended a thief using jujutsu self-defense techniques he learned in Japan. A grateful storeowner and others in the community convinced Tanaka to start a jujutsu dojo in back of the store. Original members of the dojo included Okazaki Seishiro, Nakashima Kazuo and Inouye Teruchi." Sakamoto also remembered that a "Nanpa-Shoshin Ryu Ju-Jitsu group was active in Pepeekeo with a Mr. Hamai as instructor, about 1918."

Kano's visits to Hawaii must have played a pivotal role. Sakamoto and Kawasaki stated that *circa* 1918–1923,

Shunyo Kan
judo club,
circa 1926.

USJF Archives

"many of the older jujutsu techniques had already been displaced by the more popular Kodokan Judo movement in Japan as well as in Hawaii." Although it is clear that the practice of judo served a purpose of cultural preservation for the Japanese immigrants and Japanese Americans, there may have been a purpose for Japan as well. From the Meiji Restoration onward, Japan was extremely concerned with its image to the outside world. In fact, the Japanese government attempted to prohibit lower-class citizens from emigrating to the U.S. by creating two separate types of passports, one for immigrants and the other for non-immigrant travelers.

Given the status of Kano Jigoro and Kodokan judo in Japan, it is not inconceivable that judo was considered a method by which a positive aspect of the Japanese culture could be introduced to the U.S., and as a way of improving diplomatic relations between countries. What happened during the first decade of the 1900s reveals the channels by which the Japanese method was introduced and then was to be ingrained in the mentality of U.S. citizens.

Okazaki Seishiro arrived in Hawaii at 16. There, he worked on plantations. His health was poor. Doctors diagnosed a lung disease at a pre-tubercular stage. In order to recover some health, Okazaki Seishiro decided to practice martial arts. He studied various styles including Western ones like wrestling and boxing. He later combined these systems into his own Danzan Ryu, Danzan being the kanji that denote the islands. In addition, Okazaki became a prominent figure in restoration massage in Hawaii. In many ways, Seishiro "Henri" Okazaki's life illustrates the bridges built up between Eastern and Western cultures.

Courtesy of the Kodokan Institute

1937 Nanka *Yudanshakai* judo players and U.S.A. wrestling team aboard the *Taiyo Maru* for an annual competitive tour of Japan, Korea, and Manchuria. Center row, seated, from left: Professor Yamada, Prince Konoye, Ship Captain, coach Roy Moore, Professor Yamauchi. Emilio Bruno was then a member of the American wrestling team.

FROM JUJUTSU TO JUDO

The period running from the 1920s to the late 1940s was crucial in the development of judo in the U.S. However, a clear distinction has to be made before and after Japan's surprise attack on Pearl Harbor on December 7, 1941, which forced the United States into World War II. The first decades of the 20th century saw the rooting of jujutsu into American urban culture. Progressively, more facets of the Japanese method were exposed to a wider public. A shift from self-defense to education appeared in the early 1930s, permitting the introduction of judo into new circles. However, a different speed, different means, and different goals characterize the complexity of its diffusion among Caucasian and Japanese American communities.

Courtesy of the Kodokan Institute

HEALTH AND STRENGTH

The general public did not make any difference between jujutsu and judo. Newspapers kept focusing on efficiency in personal encounters as shown in articles and book titles: "Fearful Art of Jiu-Jitsu" by Robert Edgren in *Outing*, 1905; *Ju-Jitsu, the Japanese Physical Training and Self-Defense* by Drayton, 1907; "Jiudo, the Japanese Art of Self-Defense" by Kano Jigoro in *Living Age*, 1922; "The Secrets of Jiu-Jitsu" by Otoro in *Popular Mechanics*, 1930; *Police Jiu-Jitsu and Vital Holds in Wrestling* by Futsiaka and Butch, 1937. Almost systematically the contents referred to the same extraordinary feats of Japanese experts. In 1916, an inspired journalist relating a bout held at Brown's Gymnasium in New York between Miyake Taro, a jujutsu champion residing in London, and Will Bingham, the welterweight champion of England and instructor at the New York Athletic Club, did not fear to title his paper: "If wars were waged with bare hands, if all guns

USJF Archives

Allan Corstorphin Smith, hand-to-hand fighting instructor at the Infantry School, Camp Benning, 1917–1918.

"Judo-Kodo-Kwan, Latest Japanese Game is the Most Dangerous of All: Certain Throws Mean Certain Death." In the 1920s, the image of Kano's method in the general public was still linked with self-defense.

The New York Globe, April 1921.

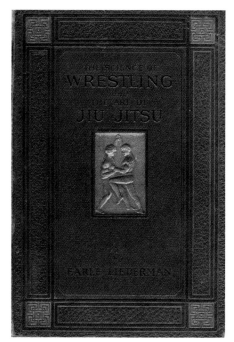

USJF Archives

and engines were banished from battle, here is the man, who, with only his wonderful strength and unequalled mastery of Jiu-Jitsu could conquer, one after the other, any man in the world—Why the "Jap" science wins." In 1918, advertisements for the book by Oshima and Yokoyama from Rikko Art Co., Cleveland, Ohio, presented jujutsu (and Kodokan judo) as "an Ideal Gift for Your Soldier."

But, the Japanese method was not just a substitute for the weak to overcome the strong. The way it was beneficial for health was regularly highlighted. Prior to the Russo-Japanese War that image was even prominent. The full title of the first book published in 1903 by Hancock was: *Japanese physical training; the system of exercise, diet, and general mode of living that has made the Mikado's people the healthiest, strongest, and happiest men and women in the world*. About 1905, the Physicians' Publishing Company from Boston issued *A Complete Course of Jiu-Jitsu and Physical Culture*. The Japanese system of training was then seen as a cure-for-all and entered daily life. Other examples could be given. In 1923, stressing once more the image of traditional Japan, The American College of Physical Culture proclaimed in *The Household Physician*: "The Japanese are the hardiest race of people in the world today, and we attribute their wonderful strength and power of endurance solely to the persistent practice of their national system of physical development. Jiu-Jitsu develops every muscle and strengthens every organ in the human body. [. . .] Jiu-Jitsu is also a natural and positive cure for constipation, indigestion, and all forms of dyspepsia, insomnia, pulmonary troubles, and lack of vitality. Its practice improves the appetite, accelerates circulation and aids assimilation. And to the increased vigor and tone of the system the brain responds, and the mental capacity as well as the physical is improved. The Japanese enjoy better health than any other nationality." Although forceful, such inflated statements are not rare. Book XIX of the *Library of Health, Complete Guide to Prevention and Cure of Disease* is dedicated to the wonders due to jujutsu. Besides pictures illustrating some maneuvers, the text deals with "jujutsu for breathing, indigestion, insomnia," and jujutsu as a "cure for obesity and pulmonary diseases."

USJF Archives

The sanitation movement that developed from the second half of the 19th century expanded with the strenuous life mystique showing the continuous run of the themes of regeneration and renewal. Health reformers like physician John Harvey Kellogg and Harvard physical education teacher Dudley Sargent altered the way Americans responded to their own bodies and culture. "Weakness is a crime. Don't be a criminal!" This famous slogan by Bernarr MacFadden, "the Father of Physical Culture," conveys the impact and the implications of the quest for health in America. From the start, jujutsu appeared of great interest for health advocates. In several European countries, physicians wrote book prefaces or gave interviews to promote health with the Japanese system of training. As in Paris with Edmond Desbonnet or in London with William "Appollo" Bankier, U.S. national and local physical culture promoters took advantage of the vogue for body exercises. They hired jujutsu teachers to enlarge their offer to the wealthy thus creating a tight connection between the Japanese system and the worlds of health and strength. A close relationship is obvious with the involvement of physical culture club owners who opened classes or promoted challenge matches. Books, articles, and advertisements were commonly published by companies or issued by magazines specialized in physical culture like MacFadden publications and encyclopedia or Spalding Athletic Library, for example. Even if minor when compared to the self-defense trend, the pro-health attitude remained constant. In the 1940s, authors kept promoting health through practice like J. C. Cogdill, in "Victory Guide"; Book on Building Health and Science of Jiu Jitsu or Frederick Paul Lowell in America Fit! with Jiu Jitsu-judo.

USJF Archives

Bernarr MacFadden,
The Encyclopedia of
Physical Culture, 1933
MacFadden's
Encyclopedia.

USJF Archives

45

FROM JUJUTSU TO JUDO

Stanislaw Cyganiewicz a.k.a. Zbysko was a professional wrestler who toured Europe and the United States during his career.

Higashi Katsukuma, who wrote several books with Irving Hancock, was less successful than Maeda or Miyake. On April 7, 1905, his fight lost in "three straight falls" against George Bothner was intensely reported by *The New York Times*: "Jiu-Jitsu *versus* the American style of wrestling was the novel entertainment provided last night for 3,000 to 4,000 spectators in the Grand Central Palace, Lexington Avenue." Under an unequivocal title, "Jiu-Jitsu Beaten by Yankee Wrestler," opponents had been brought together with a race-oriented perspective in mind. The report of the issue of the contest clearly revealed the atmosphere. "By a quick throw the Jap hurled Bothner over his shoulders. He and his judge (Irving Hancock) appealed to the referee for a flying fall. Judge O'Brien claimed that both shoulders did not touch and the referee upheld him. This aroused the ire of Higashi and for several minutes it looked as though he would not go back on the mat. Pandemonium reigned." Graham Noble, who has studied jujutsu early challenges, reported the gibes of the crowd: "A small bodyguard of Japanese came out with Higashi, and a number of their countrymen was in the crowd, one spectator remarking that there were almost enough to take Port Arthur." Reports of the match, debate on the rules, standpoints, and everything reached the same issue: the cultural supremacy of one style of wrestling.

Martin "Farmer" Burns was not only the famous wrestler who won the World wrestling title in 1895 and supposedly wrestled over 6,000 matches, but he also trained many athletes, turning one of them, the legendary Frank Gotch, into a World champion. Additionally, Farmer Burns was a creative and smart businessman. In 1912, he wrote a notorious correspondence course divided into twelve lessons that was sold all around the United States. Lesson XII deals with "Jiu Jitsu—Self Defense and Their Relation to Wrestling." He stated: "In my opinion, there is very little in the so-called Jiu-Jitsu teaching that is not included in a full and complete knowledge of catch-as-catch-can wrestling [. . .] I have personally wrestled with the greatest Japanese experts [. . .] In these contests I have invariably won without losing a simple point and this should be conclusive proof of the fact that the knowledge of American wrestling is the best of all knowledge for self protection." Such an attitude is not unique.

Individuals with an ideal body like Charles Atlas, "the world's most perfectly developed man," or Earle Liederman, "the Muscle Builder," expanded the clientele of their physical culture clubs and correspondence courses with the Japanese art. They were joined by strongmen like the famous Galen Gough, the "World's Strongest Man," who wrote "Simplified Self Defense Thru an Improved System of Americanized Jiu-Jitsu and Judo" not without declaring his method superior: "The Japanese have been masters of their system for 2,000 years. For every offensive thrust, there is also a defensive maneuver. The Japanese know the defenses of their own system, but not mine."

The Science of Ju Jitsu and Japanese Combat Tricks, Johnson & Smith Company, 1935.

Kinja Akeda, March 30, 1922. "The hold by the use of which he recently compelled Bull Montana."

However, the opposition of methods is not just a surface contradiction for marketing purposes. The contents of the courses and books are more or less the same collection of self-defense techniques. Thus titles not referring to the Japanese culture exhibit a will of appropriation by Caucasian Americans. The emergence of a new formulation like American jujutsu is not just innovative. It is also the expression of a desire to see the art become less exclusive and mass-oriented, as it appears in the very first lines of new cheap publications. Without acrimony but with a lot of hindsight, the anonymous writer of *The Science of Ju-Jitsu* declared in 1935: "Although a scientific sport in which brute strength is far outweighed by knowledge and speed, Ju Jitsu had not become something of common knowledge in America. The author believes this situation can be attributed to a number of reasons, one of them being that high prices have been asked for books and courses detailing the secrets of the science. It was the idea of getting fundamentals of Ju Jitsu to the great mass of people at moderate cost which caused the writer to offer this book at a nominal price."

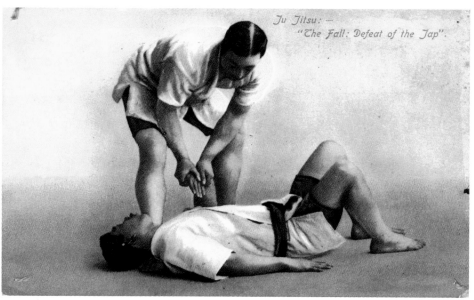

Ju Jitsu: —
"The Fall: Defeat of the Jap".

USJF Archives

"Hard-boiled Haggerty
Stops El Pulpo in Mat
Massacre," *Los Angeles
Times*, Thursday,
October 27, 1938.

*"Hard-boiled, tears in his
eyes, seemed very upset
on the fate that had
befallen El Pulpo and, just
to prove that he is a sweet
sentimentalist after all, he
stepped on the Mexican's
head as he left the ring.
Other details, which come
under the heading of
just good, clean fun: Killa
Shikuma, the Japanese
ambassador of torture,
disposed of Bob Gregory,
the British envoy, in 15m.
3s. with a Mikado Special,
known as a choke hold
to you and the Japanese
Foreign Ministry. It was a jiu
jitsu match but Gregory did
not appear to appreciate
his jacket, probably
because it did not come
with two pair of pants."*

The line that separated communities and led to disparaging responses to jujutsu in the early 1900s found a new development. For a growing number of people, jujutsu and later judo had to take some distance from its Japanese origins and be adapted to the American culture. Evidence of such a trend is obvious in some military manuals: "This school, with its roots in Tokyo, sent out branches throughout the civilized world. One branch, founded in 1921, had its headquarters in New York. It was called the New York Dojo, and while catering mainly to Japanese, admitted Occidentals who were interested. However, progress of the Occidentals were slow, due to the fact that their instruction was mainly in competitive work. The holds were ineffective because the correct principles were not taught. Very little of the defensive or protective tactics was taught. Since this was the type of judo in which the average American was interested, he soon dropped out from the school. A group of young Americans, disgusted with this procedure, set out to develop a system of self-defense suited to the American temperament and need. They called their organization 'The American Judo Club' and dedicated themselves to removing Oriental terminology from the new system. They produced as good a system as the Japanese and far outstripped in effectiveness of method. With a knowledge of American unarmed defense the American soldier will be equipped to meet the Judo men in the game which they have chosen to claim as their own." Such a position, coming from an official War Department publication, the *Basic Field Manual, Unarmed Defense for the American Soldier FM 21-150,* is most informative. It points out the gap between Caucasian

Health and Strength
by Charles Atlas,
correspondence course.

Fifteen Secrets of Jiu-Jitsu:
*"Jiu-Jitsu is the method
the sneaky Japs use to
overpower an opponent.
It is seemingly miraculous
in that it enables a weaker
person to easily subdue
one much stronger
than himself."*

and Japanese communities and provides the main key for understanding the history of judo in America.

Restricted to exclusive circles of upper-class people, to the Army and the Navy, undifferentiated jujutsu and judo were considered to be an efficient, sophisticated, and noticeably cultural means of self-defense. However, they undeniably were not part of the sports movement

Judo training in Japan, *circa* **1920.**

in America. The reluctance to admit Japanese wrestling as a cultural import was founded on several issues. High prices, the focus on secrecy, and the Oriental way of teaching were seen as the main obstacles. This might explain the incapacity of the Japanese instructors to adapt themselves to the needs and habits of the U.S. students. Even if, in some cases, xenophobic feelings turned disapproval into condemnation, these were not the only reasons why neither jujutsu nor judo benefited from the "golden age of sports" that characterized the 1920s. As in Europe, U.S. sports historians have pointed out the role of sports in the shaping of a national identity. Thus, in the United States, World War I sports training programs were pivotal in the widespread interest in sports during the 1920s. Thousands of men have been introduced to sports during their military service, most of them for the first time. Sharing a passion for plays and games they have discovered the cult of strenuousity by practicing physical activities.

At the turn-of-the-century, sports were used to distract the troops from less wholesome forms of amusement. Then, team sports were organized to strengthen bodies and patterns of socialization. More and more leaders and instructors regarded sports as a tool for the physical and social preparedness of young American men. Actually, no room was made for the Japanese art of wrestling in the mainstream of this evolution. The Army and Navy both had set up extensive wrestling and boxing programs. But, jujutsu and judo could not be considered as combat sports simply because they were not sports. Unlike in Europe, no attempt had ever been made in America in those days to establish jujutsu sporting rules nationwide. As Higashi declared to *The Cosmopolitan,* in May 1905: "Jujitsu is neither a sport nor a pastime; instead of a mat or in a sanded arena, as with wrestling, its arena is wherever an attack awaits you." In

49

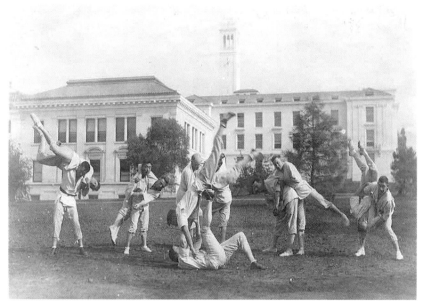

Courtesy of the University of California, Berkeley

his book, in 1918, Yamanaka, advocating Kano's method, widened the scope: "Therefore, no matter how strong your body may grow, no matter how wonderful your art of contest may be, you can never be said to have attained the real object of judo, if your character and behavior leave room for improvement." With such a perspective, recorded performances could not be a goal for practice. In addition, the political and social context with its anti-Japanese attitudes brought numerous obstacles. Lessons were included in hand-to-hand fighting courses, but having American instructors teaching Japanese techniques to large audiences was another issue. When specialized courses were given, they were aimed at special squads or combat units under certain circumstances. However, the role of the military was important in the sense that it preserved the image of efficiency and carried on its training, on a regular but limited basis.

Because of its cultural heritage the Japanese method could not raise the same enthusiasm, attract the same crowds, and epitomize the same individual and collective values as team sports did. Even in Japanese communities, sumo was far more popular and spectacular than jujutsu or judo. Because of their original functions, martial arts were self-protection or self-perfection oriented. The symbolism and dramatic character exhibited by sumo wrestlers could not be matched. No other physical activity could compare with the extraordinary power of a sumo tournament, as well as its gambling opportunities, as a social event in Pre-World War II Japanese American communities. Another vehicle that helped jujutsu and judo to spread failed. Prizefighting had its golden age prior to World War I. When team sports became popular, newspapers stopped reporting bouts between strongmen. Even if Japanese experts have always captured special attention, the interest of the general public was now focused on the stadium. As a matter of fact, the progress of the Japanese fighting art was not really slowed down among Caucasian communities. Nevertheless, compared to the huge impulse given to sports in general and to team sports in particular, it could be seen as a regression. The enthusiasm of the social elite with a passion for Japanese culture persisted. Although less embedded in the sensational press coverage, reports of the feats of experts became scarce. Exhibitions of the art were thus condemned to smaller audiences. The fame of the Japanese experts of the early 1900s did not vanish but it was blurred by the celebrity of new American sports heroes.

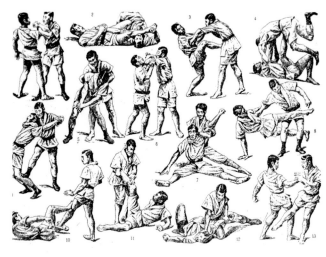

Grand Larousse Illustré,
French dictionary, 1921.

KANO, AMBASSADOR OF JUDO

Main changes occurred in the 1930s that resulted in a shift in collective representation from self-defense to physical and moral education, that is, from jujutsu to judo. It is interesting to note that a similar move is seen in Europe at the same time although in a different context. For example, in France, indirect evidence was given when the word "jiu-jitsu" was accepted by the *Grand Larousse* dictionary in 1905, the word "judo" in 1931. In the United States, such a transformation resulted from a combination of separate factors. Put together, the role of Japanese communities, an evolution in the concepts of education, and the contribution of a respected educator, Kano Jigoro, led to a new situation.

Kano was an ambassador of judo and of Japan. Despite the rigors of travels in those days, Kano came to the U.S. many times. He often made his way to Europe via Hawaii, San Francisco, Seattle, or New York, in order to promote judo in North American Japanese communities.

His visits were full of meetings, exhibitions, interviews, and dojo opening celebrations. The shift from jujutsu to judo in Japan might have been easier. In Western countries in general and in the United States in particular, various styles of jujutsu have been imported and more or less promulgated. In Japan, the Kodokan Institute could control teaching, with the support of successive regulations that made judo lessons compulsory in schools and colleges. Abroad, Kano's power of influence was undoubtedly very high. However, it was somewhat limited to Japanese communities and had no institutional framework. Kano's strategy to develop his method might have been to use the principles he advocated. Apparently, he accepted the collective representations of jujutsu instead of changing the general public's perception. He made it evolve in the direction he had chosen. This is why jujutsu and judo still looked so entwined prior to World War II. Kano astutely used the way the Japanese art of wrestling was envisioned in Western countries to establish a new system, a new network.

On the occasion of the 10th Olympiad in Los Angeles, Kano toured California and Canada. He gave several lectures. One of them, given at the University of Southern California and subsequently published in the *Journal of Health and Physical Education,* expressed the full stage of development to which Kano's thoughts had evolved since the founding of the Kodokan Cultural Association in 1922. The title Kano opted for his lecture summarized the goal of his dedication: "The Contribution of Jiudo to Education." Kano kept repeating that unlike jujutsu, judo

Courtesy of the Kodokan Institute

Kano Jigoro traveled extensively during his life. He made tireless efforts to support judo development in many Japanese communities worldwide, especially in the United States.

1912	5th Olympiad in Stockholm, Paris, London, New York, San Francisco
1920	7th Olympiad in Antwerp, Paris, London, New York, San Francisco
1932	10th Olympiad in Los Angeles, Vancouver, Seattle, Hawaii
1936	11th Olympiad in Berlin, Seattle, Vancouver, New York, Paris, London
1938	Singapore, Cairo, New York, Seattle

Los Angeles Olympic Games, 1932.

was the teaching of "maximum efficiency and mutual welfare and benefit." His motto was clear. He urged people to practice not for immediate results but in order to improve themselves and society:

"Jiudo is a study and training in mind and body as well as in the regulation of one's life and affairs. From the thorough study of the different methods of attack and defense I became convinced that they all depend on the application of one all-pervading principle, namely: 'Whatever be the object, it can best be attained by the highest or maximum efficient use of mind and body for that purpose.' Just as this principle applied to the methods of attack and defense constitutes Jiu-jitsu, so does this same principle, applied to physical, mental and moral culture, as well as to ways of living and carrying on of business, constitute the study of, and the training in, those things.

"Once the real importance of this principle is understood, it may be applied to all phases of life and activity and enables one to lead the highest and the most rational life. The real understanding of this principle need not necessarily be arrived at through the training in the methods of attack and defense, but as I came to conceive of this idea through training in these methods, I made such training in contest and the training for the development of the body the regular means of arriving at the principle.

"This principle of maximum efficiency, when applied to the keying up or perfecting of social life, just as when applied to the coordination of mind and body, in the science of attack and defense, demands, first of all, order and harmony among its members, and this can only be attained through mutual aid and concessions, leading to mutual welfare and benefit. The final aim of Jiudo, therefore, is to inculcate in the mind of man a spirit of respect for the

53

principle of maximum efficiency and of mutual welfare and benefit, leading him so to practice them that man individually and collectively can attain to the highest state, and, at the same time, develop the body and learn the art of attack and defense."

During his stay in North America, Kano devoted his time to the promotion of his art. He worked at all levels once more defining the educative goals of judo practice, but also organizing institutions, and changing names of asso- ciations. He did a lot of public-relations exercises within Japanese and non-Japanese communities, giving promotions, solving individual problems, and giving signs of his visit that are still worshipped today. His brush writings are still hanging on the walls of several dojos in Hawaii and Northern California. It is obvious that the knowledge Kano had acquired as an IOC member helped him to organize judo on an institutional basis involving individuals who were prominent in society. For instance, he pushed local judo leaders to reorganize their judo association. The Kodokan Nanka Judo Yudanshakai was thus changed into the Hokubei Judo Yudanshakai or Southern California Judo Black Belt Association of North America. Its president was the consul general of Japan. In Seattle, he urged the local judo leaders to form a black belt association, which led to the eventual creation of the Seattle Judo Yudanshakai in 1935 by Kumagai and Sakata. A Reverend Yukawa was its first president.

Other examples could be given. But, a report by Richard Bowen, who wrote the story of judo in Great Britain, highlighted Kano's policy for the development of judo in Western countries. "Saturday, 26th August 1933, at a meeting of The Budokwai's Committee, Dr Kano announced that he wished to merge the Society with the Kodokan, creating a London Branch of the Kodokan. A general meeting of the Society was called and it was agreed without dissent that The Budokwai should become a Provisional Branch of the Kodokan. The only point of disagreement was that while the members wished to retain the name Budokwai in some form Kano was not keen on this, he wanted any new entity to be known as the Kodokan, London Branch. Eventually a compromise was reached. [. . .] on Saturday, July 21st 1934, Kano convened a meeting to form a Kodokan Yudanshakai of Great Britain. [. . .] The proposal for a Kodokan Branch to take over The Budokwai ultimately collapsed, almost certainly because of the worsening international situation. But even shortly before his death in 1938 Kano was still talking about a London Branch of the Kodokan."

Los Angeles
Olympic Games,
1932.

Courtesy of the Kodokan Institute

Kano wanted an institutionalized international network with the Kodokan on top of it. Obviously, this scheme triggered reactions and not only among Westerners but also among experts in Japanese American communities. In the martial world, the complexity of the relationships between Eastern and Western Japan, that is, between the Kodokan and the Butoku Kai, was also a crucial issue that could explain divergent attitudes. The stress put on educative values by Kodokan leaders equaled the emphasis placed on martial virtues by the Butoku Kai. Thus differences appeared also in other fields like toughness of training, realism of techniques, and efficiency of fighters that raised rivalry between the two institutions. However, outside Japan antagonism did not spread out and for outsiders judo appeared as a whole. Even if Kano's ideas were prominent, such diverse trends still existed most likely among first and second generations of immigrants.

In the general public, the image of judo was more and more multi-faceted and distinct from the previous self-defense techniques. The educative approaches that were developed were not new, so to speak. In July 1905, the subtitle of Dick Merriwell's story already mentioned a difference: "Judo Art Against Jiu-Jitsu." But, distinctions appeared more regularly and above all judo was then presented as a "modern form of jujutsu." As a matter of fact, Kano's efforts to publicize his method throughout the United States started to be successful and the 1930s opened up new possibilities.

JUDO AND EDUCATION

The dates of known judo tournaments held in the Pacific Northwest between 1907 and 1942 have been listed by Joseph R. Svinth. The numbers collected are very informative: 1907–1929, 13 events; 1930–1934, 27 events; 1935–1939, 51 events. Over the years, the exposure of the Japanese method clearly became greater among Japanese and Caucasian communities. This progression raises numerous questions, the central one being what accounts for the growth of such a physical activity considering the fact it started during the Great Depression, a period during which American society experienced major economic and social difficulties. This phenomenon can be explained by two main reasons, first the increasing concern of American society for education, then the role played by sport in the Japanese communities for the double purpose of assimilation and the guarding of traditions.

The publication of *Democracy and Education,* in 1916, deeply influenced the American theories on education in general and on physical education more particularly. The primary importance of society's essence appeared as the core of the philosophy of John Dewey, who stated: "education should be a freeing of individual capacity in a progressive growth directed to social aims." Dewey's ideas had a quick and lasting impact on physical educators. In 1920, the Committee of the Society of Directors of Physical Education declared: "If the perfection of the individual in his social relations is of greater importance than purely personal values, then the first aim is the development of habits of obedience, subordination, self-sacrifice, cooperation, friendliness, a spirit of fair play, and sportsmanship." There is a strong convergence between

Courtesy of the Kodokan Institute

"*Nothing in the world is more important than education. If a teacher develops one good student, ten thousand will be influenced. One century's behaviour will affect one hundred centuries.*"

Signed "Shinkosai," Kano's pen name in his sixties.

Courtesy of the Kodokan Institute

the final assertion of Dewey's book, "all education which develops power to share effectively in social life is moral. It forms a character which not only does the particular deed socially necessary but one which is interested in that continuous readjustment which is essential to growth," and the goals of judo Kano repetitively presented during his conferences and lectures: "The actual facts prove that our society is lacking in something which, if brought to light and universally acknowledged, can remodel the society and bring greater happiness and satisfaction to this world."

In the 1930s, the conviction that social values and behavioral patterns necessary for good citizenship have to be taught through physical activities gained more and more advocates. New programs in colleges, universities, or institutions promoted sports practice and some started to include the Japanese method, especially at the Young Men's Christian Associations and later at the Young Women's Christian Associations. Kano's crusade for education benefited from the U.S. Progressive Movement in education. The once-called "bone-breaking" techniques started to be looked at differently by Caucasians.

Another part of the explanation is the pivotal role played by sports that offered the Japanese immigrant communities a way to acculturate to American society while at the same time allowing them to preserve their cultural heritage. By engaging in sports the Japanese were able to compete in a controlled environment with set rules, while at the same time exercising values such as courage, honor, commitment, and perseverance, the real signs of their cultural inheritance. This was true especially for those sports that involved either training or competition as a group or team since the collegiality and camaraderie offered by group work fit well with the group-orientation of the Japanese. As many of the Issei were getting too old to engage in sporting activities by 1930, this role of sport was especially important for the Nisei youth.

Of all sports to have an impact on the Japanese immigrant communities, none did as much as baseball. Baseball and basketball afforded the Japanese immigrants, as well as immigrants and ethnic groups from other countries, a platform meant to Americanize their communities while it also respected Japanese values. Baseball and basketball were a reassuring sign to the outside world that the Japanese had accepted the American lifestyle. However, the exact degree to which baseball and basketball were actually used for Japanese to enter the American mainstream is questionable, because their leagues were almost exclusively all Japanese. Besides, a number of traditionally Japanese sports and activities also flourished. In contrast to American-based activities, this could be understood as ways by which the Japanese communities attempted to maintain their Japanese culture and heritage. The martial arts suited the group orientation and consciousness of the Japanese communities. Dojos allowed the Japanese to expose their traditional Japanese values and attitudes. Sumo, kendo, and judo provided the Japanese with a means to express their Japaneseness. At the same time, they functioned as mechanisms by which those values, attitudes, and behaviors could be learned and reinforced in the first place. Complementing these factors is the fact that the original martial art instructors were expected to come almost exclusively from Japan, the real source of expertise and tradition. Since the purpose of these martial arts was the inculcation of values and ways of life, many in the Japanese communities thought they were the perfect vehicles by which the Issei could maintain their heritage and the Nisei could learn about it. Symbolically while baseball and basketball were seen as signs of assimilation,

Syracuse Judo Club, 1940.

Courtesy of JA Centennial Committee

58

FROM JUJUTSU TO JUDO

sumo, kendo, and judo can be understood as signs of cultural reaffirmation. The shift from jujutsu to judo occurred in Japan at the end of the 19th century. However, in the U.S., Kano had to deploy all his energy to gain a similar result in the 1930s.

THE ROOTING OF JUDO

Progressively, judo organizations in the U.S. developed in the main cities of the country, principally those where Japanese communities were established. After the rooting of judo in the Seattle, San Francisco, Los Angeles, and Hawaii areas a number of dojos sprung up all around the northwest in Washington, Oregon, and California (especially the central part where there were many farming communities). For example, before World War II, six dojos were numbered in Oregon, the strongest in the Portland area being the Shobukan dojo. In the early 1930s, judo was taught in Denver by two instructors named Ito and Fukumoto. At the same time in Chicago judo was practiced sporadically by members of the Japanese consulate and other interested individuals. The first judo club in Chicago was opened by a Harry Auspitz in 1938, as the Jiu Jitsu Institute. Afterward, several other dojos opened in that area prior to World War II. Judo had grown and progressed to the point that dojos formed regional organizations to coordinate and cooperate in their activities. For example in 1925, the Kodokan issued the first black belts to judo players in Hawaii, and in 1928, the three largest Hawaiian clubs—Shobukan, Shunyokan, and

Kano Jigoro planting a commemorative tree at the Hawthorn national language academy in the suburbs of Los Angeles, 1932.

Courtesy of the Kodokan Institute

FROM JUJUTSU TO JUDO

In New York, judo was first introduced at the Nippon Athletic Club in 1916. The New York Judo Club opened in 1919, and later its instructors were George Gensuke Yoshida and Kawaishi Mikinosuke. When Kawaishi left, the New York Judo Club and the Nippon Athletic Judo Club merged to form the New York Dojo, and from this time George Yoshida was largely responsible for the maintenance of judo standards and development in the area. He was given the right to issue Kodokan dan grades by Kano Jigoro directly. Yoshida had an extraordinary position because only he had exclusive dan granting power until 1960 when the New York Yudanshakai was founded.

1936 Geo. Yoshida

Kano at a 1936 New York Dojo promotion contest.

Courtesy of Mel Appelbaum

Hawaii Chugakko—organized judo in the territory. They formed the Hawaii Judo Association. Similarly, in 1928, the judo leaders in the Los Angeles area founded the Nanka Judo Yudanshakai or Southern California Judo Black Belt Holders Association.

During each of his stays in the U.S., Kano made continuous efforts to implement official judo structures related to the Kodokan. When he attended the Los Angeles Games, he must have viewed them as the culmination of his own ideas about the social and cultural impact of sport practice. For the first time in the history of the Olympic Games, events were concentrated over a short period of time. It set off the magnitude of these Games. The record crowds, with 100,000 people attending the opening ceremony at the Memorial Coliseum, proved the growing place of sports in society, and the importance of its values. The success of the Olympic movement in the United States confirmed for Kano the necessity of his educational quest. His 1932 two-month visit gave him the opportunity to multiply contacts, lectures, and meetings. Having been in Vancouver on August 17, 1932, for judo purposes, Kano gave a speech the day after in Tacoma to the Japanese Language School Teachers' Assembly of the Northwest. Once more his chosen theme was the role of judo in education. Consul Uchiyama Kiyoshi also gave a lecture. The gist of Kano's speech was that the Nisei needed to learn what Japanese language schools taught if they were to be able to properly interpret Japan for the benefit of Americans of European stock. On August 19, Kano gave a similar speech to the Japan Society of Seattle.

On August 20, 1932, Kano went south, visited the Portland area, and renamed the Shobukan judo club Obukan, which still exists today under longtime leader Jim Onchi. That night he drove back to Seattle to give a speech at the Nippon Kan theater, a major social venue in that time period. In that speech Kano said that the Nisei "must first of all be taught to become genuine and good American citizens. The ideal of world peace and mankind's welfare must always be kept before them." In a Seattle community newspaper he underscored that "Americans of Japanese ancestry could only fulfill their proper part in their country's national life by becoming genuine citizens." The day after, Kano attended a judo tournament in Seattle and approved some promotions, including one for *nidan* to Ken Kuniyuki, who later became one of the founding fathers of the U.S. Judo Federation and a leader in Southern California. Kano then traveled by train to San Francisco, where he encouraged another local *yudanshakai*. This led to the creation of Hokka Judo Yudanshakai, Northern California Judo Black Belt Association.

On his way back to Japan, Kano visited Hawaii. This was an auspicious visit because in 1932, the Hawaii Judo Kyokai received official recognition by the Kodokan as the first official *yudanshakai* outside of Japan (certificate #76 issued by the Kodokan on November 15, 1932), granting promotion authority to Hawaii. This authority with a direct line to the Kodokan was the only such line granted outside of Japan for decades. Today in the U.S., Kodokan rank is authorized under the auspices of the U.S.-Kodokan committee, which is the only such committee of its kind in the world to share such a relationship with the Kodokan. In 1933, the name of Hawaii Judo Kyokai was changed to Hawaii Judo Yudanshakai—the Judo Black Belt Federation of Hawaii, which still exists today.

Kano made similar efforts in July 1936 when he came to Seattle during his travels for the Berlin Olympics. On his way back to Japan from Germany, he visited with the Japanese community in Los Angeles. On October 23, he

Hawaiian hospitality.

61

Judo sensei in front of Yamauchi's home. With Professor Kotani, Professor Yoshida, Professor Yamauchi, and Professor Iida.

Gardena, California, 1932.

attended a dinner at the Kawafuku restaurant in Los Angeles. Kano watched the judo tournament between the Northwest all-stars against the Southern California all-stars, and bestowed promotions among some individuals, including a *sandan* for Tamura Masato.

Kano's last visit to America came during his return to Japan from an Olympic meeting in Cairo in 1938. After a stop in New York City, he took a plane bound to Chicago and Seattle. On the evening of April 20, he watched the promotional tournament of the Seattle judo association held at Washington Hall. Fife's Iwakiri Ryoichi received promotion to 3-dan while his fourteen-year-old son George Makoto received promotion to 1st dan. Future U.S. Judo Federation president and IJF Medical Commissioner Koiwai Eichi was also promoted during this tournament.

As judo grew and organizations were created, organized competitions were also conducted. In the 1930s, for instance, the dozen or so dojos in the greater Seattle area each sponsored a judo tournament during the four or five winter months. Judo teams in Washington competed regularly against their counterparts in Vancouver and against Japanese naval training ship teams and college teams. Similar goodwill matches were held with Japanese naval training ships wherever they berthed, such as Hawaii, San Francisco, and Los Angeles as well. At least in Hawaii, that practice continues till this day. The Southern California Judo Championships were held twice a year, in the spring and fall, and in between, clubs would compete against each other. One of the largest competition rivalries was started in the 1930s, pitting judo players in the Northwest against players from Southern California. Twice a year, 35 or so of the best judo players in the Northwest were selected by Kumagai sensei to represent their area in the annual competition with the all-stars from Southern California. The Northwest

Courtesy of Emilio Bruno

alternated with Southern California in sending their teams to the other's area for competition. Indeed, this was the only inter-regional competition that occurred during that time. Local judo players would vie for top honors at the various local tournaments in order to be selected to represent their area in the competition. Thus many judo players worked hard to gain the pride and privilege of representing their area in this rivalry, which further served to solidify and consolidate the various judo activities. During the first contest, Kenneth Kuniyuki was captain of the Northwest team, while T. Hagio was captain of the Southern California team. Seattle won that first year in the point contest, but lost in the Red and White contest (*kouhaku*, in which the winner stays up and the team with players remaining wins). The Northwest team won the next two times they competed, however, and players from the Northwest won the individual trophies three times.

It was also during the late 1930s that intercollegiate judo competition had its start. With more Nisei attending colleges and universities, judo teams began to emerge on the college level. In the 1930s, one of the leaders of organized judo in the U.S., Henry Stone, was a judo coach at the University of California, Berkeley. Cal students regularly competed at local tournaments in the San Francisco Bay Area. In 1937, Emilio (Mel) Bruno introduced judo as a sport to San Jose State College (currently the California State University at San Jose, or more colloquially San Jose State University) Physical Education Department. In 1940, Bruno and Stone conducted the first intercollegiate judo tournament in the U.S. In 1941, Bruno left San Jose to become an instructor in the Gene Tunney Fitness Program, which prepared soldiers for military duty.

TIMELINE

Dec. 7, 1941	Pearl Harbor
Feb. 19, 1942	Executive Order 9066
Mar. 24, 1942	First series of "exclusion orders"; mass incarceration of all West Coast Japanese Americans
Oct. 30, 1942	All Japanese American detainees transferred to 10 permanent War Relocation Authority detention camps called "Assembly Centers"
Feb. 8, 1943	Loyalty questionnaire administered in all 10 camps to men and women over the age of 17. The questionnaire is used to issue leaves to go outside of camps, and to segregate those whose answers were deemed unacceptable to authorities
April 1943	Volunteers from camps and Hawaii form the 442nd Regimental Combat Team, which became the most decorated unit for its size and length of service in U.S. military history
July 1943	Tule Lake designated center for those who answered "no-no" to questions #27 and #28
Jan. 20, 1944	Draft reinstated Japanese Americans
Mar.—June, 1944	Heart Mountain Fair Play Committee: 400 Nisei vote to resist draft until their constitutional rights are restored. Eighty-five are sentenced to three years in prison; 267 from all 10 camps are eventually convicted for draft resistance
Aug. 14, 1945	U.S. drops first atomic bomb on Hiroshima. Three days later, U.S. drops second atomic bomb on Nagasaki. World War II ends
Sept. 4, 1945	Western Defense Command revokes all West Coast exclusion orders against Japanese Americans
Mar. 20, 1946	Tule Lake "segregation center" closes, last of 10 camps
Dec. 24, 1947	President Truman grants pardon to all 267 Japanese American draft resisters
July 12, 1948	President Truman signs "Evacuation Claims Act." Claimants eventually paid less than 10 cents on the dollar
Sept. 1951	Japan signs peace treaty with U.S. Japan regains independence
1976	President Ford rescinds Executive Order 9066

Source: National Japanese American Historical Society

RELOCATION CENTERS

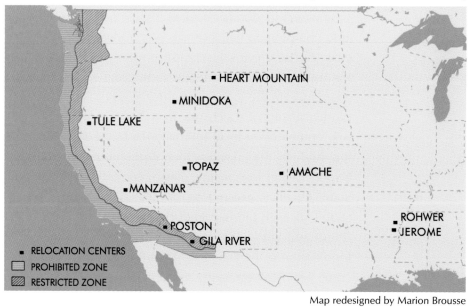

Map redesigned by Marion Brousse

The judo program having a void, Bruno asked then student Uchida Yoshihiro to take it over, teaching police students. Uchida took the first group of college judo competitors from San Jose to Southern California to participate in a Yudanshakai tournament. In 1940, Uchida also started the San Jose Buddhist Judo Club. The judo programs at San Jose State and the San Jose Buddhist Judo Club, however, were stopped when World War II broke out and Uchida was drafted. San Jose State was restarted in 1946 by Uchida, and the San Jose Buddhist Judo Club in 1947 under the direction of Don "Moon" Kikuchi.

JAPANESE CAMPS

By Executive Order 9066, President Roosevelt authorized the Secretary of War "*to prescribe military areas in such places and of such extent as he or the appropriate Military Commanders may determine, from which any or all persons may be excluded, and with such respect to which, the right of any person to enter, remain in, or leave shall be subject to whatever restrictions the Secretary of War or the appropriate Military Commander may impose in his discretion.*"

In 1939, Germany had begun its aggression against Europe by invading Poland. In the East, Japan had similarly begun its aggression with the Manchurian Incident in 1931, their withdrawal from the League of Nations in 1933, and the outbreak of war with China in 1937. In 1940, Japan signed a tripartite alliance with Germany and Italy.

Diplomatic relations between the U.S. and Japan had become increasingly strained during those years, and the U.S. placed economic sanctions against Japan in response to its aggressive actions. Finally, on December 7, 1941, the Japanese navy attacked a sleeping U.S. navy at Pearl Harbor, Hawaii, launching the U.S. into World War II. On December 8, 1941, President Roosevelt signed an executive order concerning "enemy aliens" restricting their rights and mobility. Germans and Italians were treated fairly but Japanese suffered gross injustices and discrimination.

Lobbyists from western states representing economic interests or nativist groups put strong pressure on Congress, fearing a Japanese invasion with Japanese Americans allegedly ready to strike as a 5th column. President

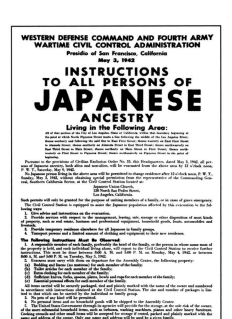

USJF Archives

Roosevelt capitulated, signing Executive Order 9066, on February 19, 1942. In the next 6 months, approximately 120,000 men, women, and children of Japanese ancestry were moved to assembly centers and then to internment camps. All lost their personal liberties; most lost their homes and properties as well.

The Japanese Americans were interned in two types of camps. Ten camps were administered by the War Relocation Authority (WRA). Although euphemistically referred to as "relocation centers," essentially they were concentration camps where Japanese Americans forcibly removed from their homes and businesses were isolated, fenced, and guarded. The 10 camps included Topaz in central Utah, Poston and Gila River in Arizona, Amache in Colorado, Heart Mountain in Wyoming, Jerome and Rohwer in Arkansas, Manzanar and Tule Lake in California, and Minidoka in Idaho.

Nisei were nevertheless encouraged to serve in the armed forces. Some were drafted. Segregated battalions from Hawaii and the mainland were formed. Due to their outstanding bravery and the heavy combat duty they faced, the 100th Infantry Battalion and the 442nd Regimental Combat Team became the most decorated units in U.S. military history relative to size and length of service: over 18,000 individual decorations for bravery and 9,500 Purple Hearts.

Despite their exploits, World War II veterans of Japanese ancestry were welcomed home by racist signs and attitudes. In many cases, they were denied service in local shops and restaurants. Their homes and property were often vandalized or set on fire.

Several thousand other Japanese Americans came under the jurisdiction of the Justice Department in a separate and parallel internment. The Justice Department's camps designated as internment camps were created for the purpose of detaining "enemy aliens." The roots of this program are found in the surveillance of the Japanese American com-

Japanese American Museum

munities carried out by various government agencies. Prior to 1940, at the request of the Justice Department's Special Defense Unit Japanese communities along the West Coast had been placed under the intense scrutiny of the FBI. To define potentially dangerous individuals, three categories had been established. Leaders with strong Japanese ties, like judo or kendo teachers, were placed on the A list. By the time of the attack on Pearl Harbor, the government kept lists of such individuals deemed dangerous. By the evening of December 8, 1941, 736 Issei leaders were held in local jails, transported north, or placed under a rigidly enforced curfew. By the next day 1,771 "enemy aliens" were in the custody of U.S. authorities, and 1,212 were of Japanese ancestry. All were Issei community leaders, including church leaders, Japanese association officials, Japanese language school principals, newspaper editors, and instructors of judo and kendo clubs. They were held in internment camps in Crystal City, Texas; Santa Fe, New Mexico;

Seagoville, Texas; Fort Stanton, New Mexico; Fort Missoula, Minnesota; Fort Lincoln, North Dakota; Kenedy, Texas; and Kooskia, Idaho. According to Justice Department records, 5,264 Japanese Americans were in custody in this program in 1945; 153 diplomats and 1,573 others had been sent back to Japan.

In addition to the Japanese Americans who were incarcerated in either concentration camps run by the WRA or internment camps run by the Justice Department, a small number of Japanese Americans were excluded and restricted but not incarcerated. These were individuals who had either moved from or were already outside the exclusion zones prior to Executive Order 9066. The local Japanese American community in Ontario, Oregon, home of the largely successful Ore-Ida Judo Club that started after the war, for instance, is such an example. According to the WRA in 1946, there were 1,963 voluntary excludees in Colorado, 1,519 in Utah, 305 in Idaho, 208 in eastern Washington, 115 in eastern Oregon, and others scattered throughout the U.S.

The WRA attempted to create camp communities that resembled normal communities to the greatest extent possible. Thus, each camp had schools and hospitals, a newspaper, some degree of democratic self government, and leisure activities such as baseball and movies. And for many of the Nisei who were very young when they moved to camp, they even report that camp life was "fun" because life was so carefree. But, of course, life in camp was anything but normal, especially for the Issei and Nisei who were old enough to see their lives uprooted. The camps were surrounded by barbed wire and armed guards. Although the guards were posted supposedly for the internees' protection, their guns were mainly pointed on the

Kilauea Military Camp, May 25, 1942, by George Hoshida.

George Hoshida worked for the Hilo Electric Light Company. He was also involved in his Buddhist temple and had a keen interest in judo. Due to his involvement Hoshida was considered "potentially dangerous" after the bombing of Pearl Harbor. Although he professed little interest in international politics, the practice of his Buddhist faith, his leadership in his temple, and his interest in judo deemed him "suspicious." Hoshida was first incarcerated in the Kilauea Military Camp in Hawaii, and then taken to the Justice Department camps at Fort Sam Houston, Lordsburg, and Santa Fe.

Japanese American Museum

67

DIARY OF JUDO PLAYERS AT TULE LAKE

By Tomita Shigeo

The first thing I learned in judo was ukemi, in order to avoid getting hurt after being thrown. Then I learned different types of throwing techniques. When I first got thrown my head would hit the tatami and it would hurt, but after practicing for two weeks it was amazing that my head would no longer hurt. Also when my partner would apply a foot sweep, I would complain that it hurt, but that just made them do more foot sweeps to bully me.

I think that I have been complaining that I hurt all the time since the new year started. When I really think about it I am glad that I was in the children's section because there are many people who are skilled and who teach me different techniques. They also threw me a lot, so now my body is stronger.

I like judo, but sometimes when I don't go to judo my mother really scolds me. Just the other night I rested from judo, and my mother said, "Don't rest for even one night. Practicing judo will help you become a fine person, and it is all for your sake, not anyone else's." I think that once you rest it is easy to do it again, and so the difference from the really good people will get greater. That's why I decided to practice judo harder than the rest of the students.

It will be one year already since starting judo.

Because our teachers try so hard to help us become fine people, I want to work my hardest so I can become a sankyu, and pay back sensei's kindness.

By Ueda Takashi

Recently I started going to judo practice with a friend. I had learned it previously, but if you don't continue it you won't get any stronger. Also my hips hurt a lot.

Recently my sensei had thrown me, and when he did it really hurt. So I really thought that if you don't practice hard your body will hurt.

I really love judo. I think that if a Japanese man doesn't know judo it is shameful. When you learn judo your body becomes strong, and if you go to war you won't lose.

The reason why Japanese military is so strong is because they learn judo or kendo from when they are small. I want to learn judo so I can become a strong Japanese military person myself.

By Hamada Hiroshi

I began judo in May. I enrolled on 18 May. The night before my father asked me whether I wanted to practice judo, but I told him that because I didn't have a judogi that I would do it another day. "If that's the case," he replied, "then you should go tonight, stop playing around, and watch and learn." When my father wasn't looking I played around and got scolded.

That night when we were going home after practice, my father said "goodbye" to the sensei. Then he taught me that I should bow towards the head of the dojo when I was leaving the dojo.

The Bancroft Library, University of California, Berkeley

Harai goshi at Rohwer Relocation Center, November 25, 1942. Photograph by Tom Parker.

I went to practice the next night. Because I didn't have a judogi, I took out the knife and pencil from my pockets and practiced in my regular clothes.

Everyone lined up in two or three lines, and after warming up, I practiced ukemi. After practice finished I went home, and when I arrived there I was so surprised to see my mother working hard to make me a judogi. Two weeks later my new judogi was ready. I will practice judo really hard, just as my mother worked so hard to make my judogi.

By Yoshimasa Takao

Manners and etiquette are really important parts of budo. When I first went to judo, I learned from the sensei that when you enter or leave the dojo, you turn towards the front of the dojo and bow. In that way we gradually learn the techniques from our sensei, and after a week I was promoted to yonkyu. Because that was the first time I was promoted I was really happy from my heart. Sensei always says that judo is really not just for yourself, but also for the betterment of society. I thought, "ah I see," when he explained it to me. Whether I go to my ancestral land of Japan or wherever I go, judo is always useful. If I think this way I feel like I really want to go. I feel like practicing twice a week is just not enough.

Because I had final exams recently, I rested from judo, but from now I plan to practice hard and faithfully. And, when I can finally go to Japan there will be no problems if I first train my mind and body, and perfect my technique.

中村幸雄

西本浩次

Courtesy of Jerry Hays

Judo on board Japanese cruiser *Atago*, sunk on October 23, 1944, during the battle of the Palawan Passage by *USS Darter*.

inside, and in fact there were several incidents of guards shooting inmates in both the concentration and internment camps.

Conflicts within the Japanese American community were exacerbated by the close confinement and bad conditions of the camps. These conflicts at times boiled over, leading to disturbances such as the Manzanar Incident and the Poston Strike. In Manzanar, where 10,000 people lived in a one square mile area, a Peace Committee was formed in the wake of the violence surrounding the Manzanar Incident. Actually this was a spontaneous arbitration and control group of interned judo players led by Seigoro Murakami, who had been a judo instructor and Japanese language school teacher before evacuation and had organized a judo instruction program in the camp. At first the only job for the Peace Committee was to maintain order at dances. Later their responsibilities expanded to include handling family differences, assaults, and other social problems. To this day the USJF Jr. National Championships annually award a Murakami trophy in honor of this judo leader for his efforts in developing judo in the Southern California area.

Most important, however, were the conflicts that emerged over Japanese roots, tradition, and heritage *versus* Americanism and American loyalty. One of the major reasons why these conflicts came to a head was that family dynamics were drastically changed. The Issei saw their authority uprooted while the Nisei gained power with newfound freedom. The crowded conditions and group living quarters undermined the hierarchical, patriarchal nature of the Japanese culture. Women began to work outside their homes. The camps violated Japanese values of privacy, patience, dignity, and self-respect.

The changing cultural and family dynamics that were forced upon the Japanese American internees exacerbated the already growing tensions in the community between the old traditions of Japan and the new assimilation of the American ways. For many people the internment sparked an intensification of cultural and ethnic identity among the Japanese Americans.

The camps were blind to such differences as citizenship, class, age, politics, or religion. Thus, the only thing that bound people together were their Japanese ancestry and heritage. Many who considered themselves primarily Americans came into contact with Japanese traditions for the first time. Festivals, ceremonies, music, folklore, courting, and other ethnic aspects of having Japanese roots were shared and strengthened.

JUDO IN THE CAMPS

C amp Harmony, located on the Seattle fair-grounds, served as the collection area for the Japanese Americans in the Seattle area from April to September 1942. Most of the judo players in the Northwest area gathered there and, searching for some semblance of order and normalcy, resumed their judo practices daily.

The Santa Anita racetrack in Los Angeles served as another assembly area from May to October 1942. It housed over 19,000 individuals. Mits Kimura, later to become one of the founding fathers of organized American judo, served as the police chief at the center and helped to start judo classes. At one time there were upward of 125 students, 30 of them women, and three practices a day. The Portland Assembly Center is reported to have had around 340 practicing members.

Sports had an important role in the social and community lives in the camp. Baseball, basketball, and volleyball games often played before packed crowds of

The Bancroft Library, University of California, Berkeley

A judo class at Heart Mountain Relocation Center, Wyoming, November 25, 1942. Judo classes were held every afternoon and evening.

71

thousands were very popular as the internees struggled to make the best of their camp life. Sports and other recreational activities actually thrived to a larger degree than before the war, mostly because of the forced idleness the new situation implied. It made life more bearable and lifted people's morales.

While American sports succeeded, so did the Japanese arts of judo, kendo, and sumo. Of course no one knew in which camp they or others would end up. But once in camp, people who did judo found each other, often by accident, and agreed to get judo going in the camp. Hank Ogawa, one of the leaders of judo in the Northwest area after the war, stated that judo got started at Topaz when he and a few other judo players got together and decided to convert one of the barracks into a dojo. At first they had no *tatami*, so they used sawdust on the floors to cushion the falls. Later, however, *tatami* were donated from the outside. At Manzanar, sawdust was covered by canvas, and the club reportedly had around 350 members. Although there were organized judo competitions, judo players mainly participated in judo for the sake of judo practices. Sumo was different. Matches played before very large audiences were often held on Sundays. In fact, they were a way to make money because spectators would pool their resources to provide for the winners of the matches. Strong sumo players could make as much as $70 or $80 a weekend, a great deal more than the $12 a month the internees received from the U.S. government to work in the service jobs within the camps.

The Bancroft Library, University of California, Berkeley

The legend of this picture taken on January 7, 1943, by Tom Parker reads: "Mrs. Kinoshida, the Russian wife of a center minister of Japanese ancestry, throws a male instructor in a Judo class at the Heart Mountain Relocation Center."

From Jujutsu to Judo

Judo played a singular role. It was not a spectator or a gambling sport. People favored other aspects like fitness, community values, and self-protection. As a Japanese art, judo served to introduce many Japanese Americans to their Japanese roots, or to reaffirm an already existing cultural identity as one rooted in Japan. Judo, with its roots in Japanese traditions, customs, and philosophy, was a perfect activity for cultural reaffirmation.

The internment experience is a turning point in the history of judo in the United States. Its effects can be appreciated from both a cultural and a structural point of view. First, judo has enforced its role as a means of educating young generations, of transmitting a national cultural heritage. In so difficult a period, judo appeared as a cultural shelter and a way to strengthen social ties. As a side effect, the specificity of its origins and the stress put on values increased the distance between the method of Kano and the contest-oriented American sports. Japanese community members proved their abilities to incorporate U.S. society usages, for example by adopting American sports. However, the large-scale anti-Japanese racist attitudes incited Japanese Americans to protect the cultural identity

Ink portraits, at Lordsburg Justice Department Camp, New Mexico, August 5, 1942, by George Hoshida.

Left, Nishii Kosa, 41-year-old missionary for the San Diego Buddhist Church, originally from Kumamoto, Japan.

Hoshida was acutely aware of the importance of recording his experiences through the pen and ink drawings and watercolors he made during his incarceration in five different locations. While Hoshida did not attempt to make any overt commentary on the internment, his drawings and sketches provide a continuous and detailed account of daily activities and his long journey from Hilo, Hawaii, to the desert of Arizona.

Right, Mochizuki Goro, 39-year-old judo and kendo instructor of Portland, Oregon, originally from Shizuoka, Japan.

73

CAMP HARMONY NEWS LETTER

Camp Harmony News Letter, Vol. 1 No. 4, May 23, 1942

Camp sports program gathers momentum.

Camp Harmony's program is well under way now, according to Chick Uno, Camp Athletic Director. Area A has started a regular intersectional softball league with a few games already played.

The setup for the entire camp will probably follow the same pattern as that in "A." Softball, class A, will be open to all. Class B will be for class A second teams and class C for those 16 years and under. The girls will also form leagues.

With Saki Arai as head man, Area "D" can expect a good athletic program in the near future. So far, he has outlined an intersectional softball league, ping pong tournaments, boxing, horseshoe-pitching, and judo.

Arai plans to have the intersectional softball champs of the different areas play for the camp title at the end of the season. However, this will depend on orders from the WCCA office.

If a few more sets of tables were available, ping pong would be in full swing, Arai reported yesterday.

Judo can get under way as soon as the mats are distributed, Uno said. In Area "A" there are four capable instructors in Maniw, Nitta, Shinoda, and Kuniyuki.

There is also a possibility that a miniature golf course will be set up to keep golfers from getting too rusty.

Camp Harmony News Letter, Vol. 1 No. 7, June 17, 1942

The first issue of the *Camp Harmony News Letter* was edited on May 5. It ended with a Souvenir Edition on August 14, 1942.

Sports. Inter-area softball slated.

Inter-area sports competition, a subject which has been brewing for the past week or so, will blossom out into a thing of reality.

For as soon as weather permits, a picked softball squad from Area B will invade Area A to play a double header. Led by Area Athletic Officer Tomeo Takayoshi the B team includes the following: T. Kurimoto, H. Kiga, M. Hayashi, Y. Tsuji, W. Yanagimachi, W. Ihashi, T. Osaka, S. Takeuchi, M. Ozaki, Ed Kiyohara, A. Aratani, B. Kinoshita, G. Kimura, Y. Sagami, S. Sagami, P. Kozu, J. Asahara, K. Okada, M. Uchida, S. Ogasawara, H. Nishimura, S. Hokari, J. Tachiyama, and T. Takayoshi.

If this inter-area experiment proves successful others may follow, Chick Uno, camp athletic officer announced yesterday. Thus far, softball, judo, basketball and boxing have been OK'd by WCCA officials as approved inter-area sports.

Camp Harmony News Letter, Vol. 1 No. 10, July 18, 1942

Judo tournament slated for 25th.

Judo's big day will come one week hence, July 25, when a promotional tourney will be held in Area D's sumo pit, Athletic Director "Chick" Uno said today.

This tournament is for those under sho-dan who will have a chance to advance themselves.

Also on the program will be special matches bringing together the senior division matmen.

With the exception, possibly of C, which has limited athletic facilities, each area will have a chance to sponsor an inter-area tourney.

Courtesy of the
Washington University
Press

**The remains of
the Manzanar
dojo.**

By Patrick Keelaghan, From the *Budokwai Quarterly Bulletin,* April to January 1946

In August [1944] when I had my week's vacation I and another lad went up to the [Manzanar] Relocation Center (pardon me, Center), some 250 miles from here [Los Angeles], where the Japanese or nisei are interned (they are the American-born, loyal element), and there we stayed the week in the nearby town [either Independence or Lone Pine], driving out every day for about an hour's judo with the internees. However, on the second day we decided to go fishing during the afternoon when there was no judo, and nothing would satisfy us but we would do some sunbathing. I think we were out for about two or three hours, and since the camp is near the desert you can imagine how hot it was. Naturally, I got sunburned, and had to give up the judo. When my blisters had somewhat subsided, I tried a go at the judo and nearly got my back torn off, so I had to give up altogether. On the Sunday we were to go home a group of the club members drove up and they held a Shiai, to grade us all, and of course I didn't want to miss that. I had myself all tied up in bandages like a mummy, and when the time came who did I get to murder me but the fellow I met the last time I was there in contest, and he had thrown me, so you can imagine how happy I was!!! Anyway, it wasn't as bad as I thought, because after a little bit of rough housing I got him with the Inner Thigh throw, unintentionally I must add, for I tried for Haraigoshi and he side-stepped into it. Then they gave me another toughie and he got me in a hold-down, just when I had forgotten about the sunburn and was getting really warmed up. However, they gave me a first Kyu to keep me quiet, and when I looked at my shoulders, which had lost all the skin, I was going to ask them for more, but I am well pleased with what I got. So I am since August [1944] a Brown Belt, and strut around now fit to kill.

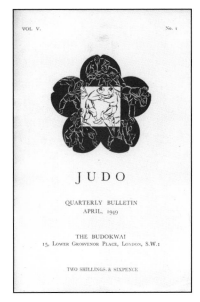

VOL. V.   No. 1

JUDO

QUARTERLY BULLETIN
APRIL, 1949

THE BUDOKWAI
15, LOWER GROSVENOR PLACE, LONDON, S.W.1

TWO SHILLINGS & SIXPENCE

of their codes and practices. Considering this, judo could not be seen as "westernizable." The way the method of Kano was traditionally taught in Japan was the only way acceptable by Japanese sensei without introducing moral transgression. Life in camps saw the beginnings of a changing of leadership between Issei and Nisei. However, the black years deeply marked the whole judo community.

On a different level, the relocation years introduced main structural changes. It contributed to the emergence of a national judo network. Before World War II, the beginning of judo organizations, mainly due to Kano's efforts, was geographically restricted. Because of the camps, many of the judo players were all of a sudden thrust together. As such they had the opportunity to know many of their counterparts who came from different areas of the country. Forming such relationships and gaining a perspective on judo outside of their own hometowns helped plant the seeds in the minds of judo leaders of a nationwide judo organization. Had the internment experience not occurred, the U.S. Judo Federation might have been created even later than it was.

Besides this, the release of the internees led to the spreading of judo throughout the country. For the vast majority of Japanese Americans in camps, however, it was not until 1945 toward the end of the war when they began to be released. Although freedom was sweet, it was for sure bittersweet, because most Japanese Americans had nowhere to go. They had lost their possessions, land, homes, and businesses when they were forced to relocate. In many instances many families had had only a day to pack whatever they could take with them to camp. And while some families had American friends who were nice enough to watch their things for them while they were in camp, most did not. So release from the camps raised disturbing questions for many of the internees. In fact, more than a few of the internees, especially some of the older Issei, didn't even know where to go and had to be forced away after the war was over. The last camp to close was the one in Crystal City, Texas, which shut its gates on February 27, 1948.

Thus while many of the Japanese American internees returned to the West Coast, some of them just ventured into new cities and communities on their own, trying to find jobs to make a living.

Others took advantage of opportunities offered to them by family, friends, or connections. Regardless, many Japanese Americans needed to scrape and scratch to make a

The Bancroft Library, University of California, Berkeley

living, finding new jobs, especially in a postwar atmosphere
in which many American businesses and businesspeople
still held anti-Japanese sentiments because of the war.

AFTER THE WAR

During the war, handfuls of Japanese Americans
were allowed to attend colleges or universities in
inland areas, such as Chicago or Denver. Some
of them were released from camps, especially those who
were determined to be "loyal" according to the loyalty
questionnaire administered by the U.S. government in the
camps. Others, however, had lived in non-exclusion areas
to begin with, and could complete their university degrees
during the war, although these were very few in number.

Obtaining their university degrees helped the Japanese American communities to re-assimilate back into the
mainstream American society faster. Many became civic
and social leaders, like Hiro Fujimoto, who obtained his
degree from Wayne State University in 1948, moved to
Detroit, and later founded the Detroit Judo Club, one of
the most successful judo clubs in the country during the

77

The Chicago Judo Club.

USJF Archives

1950s and 1960s. Actually Fujimoto was a student at UCLA but was forced to stop his studies there because of the war and internment.

The spreading of judo in the communities after the war coincided with the slow but increasingly open expression of ethnic pride and confidence on the part of the Japanese Americans. Many factors contributed to this newfound pride and confidence, among which was the very fact that they had endured the internment experience with not one individual being convicted of a crime against the government, thereby proving their loyalties as American citizens. The reputation of Nisei soldiers who acted as interpreters during the war was also a source of pride for the Japanese American communities.

Another major factor that contributed to the postwar assimilation of the Japanese American communities was the return of the 442nd Regimental Combat Team and the 100th Infantry Battalion veterans. Although the government's plan had been to recruit a total of 4,500 volunteers, over 11,000 Japanese Americans volunteered. Starting on June 26, 1944, the 442nd saw their first action, and in 225 days of combat the 442nd compiled an impressive battle record, suffering the highest casualty rate and becoming the most decorated unit for its size and length of service in American military history. Their exploits served as great propaganda for efforts to repeal the Alien Land Laws and other discriminatory legislation that existed. Many 442nd veterans came to play important civic and social roles, such as Daniel Inouye, who later became a U.S. Senator from Hawaii. The redress bill passed by the House of Representatives and the U.S. government was called H. R. 442 in honor of the 442nd.

YAMAUCHI SENSEI

USJF Archives

On June 14, 1968, the Japanese government, through Emperor Hirohito, presented to Professor Yamauchi Toshitaka the Order of the Sacred Treasure Medal for his contribution to the development of the sport of judo in the United States of America.

Born in 1894, Yamauchi Toshitaka started judo at the age of 13 at the local high school. Two years later, in 1909, he registered at the Kodokan Institute. From 1913 to 1917, he attended the Higher Teachers College of Tokyo where he majored in physical education and judo philosophy. Being dispatched by Kano to America, Yamauchi came to Los Angeles in 1917 and started teaching at Rafu dojo. Then he went to Chicago and New York where he stayed for nine years. In 1928, Yamauchi helped organize Nanka *yudanshakai*. He constantly sought to improve judo in the California area where he established several dojos. One of his early students remembers his first dojo that "started in somebody's house and later moved to a 100 x 30 foot garage. He also had a judo club in a converted dance hall." On four occasions before World War II Yamauchi led a group on a visit to Tokyo and other cities in Japan to stimulate interest and strengthen the ties between U.S. judo players and their Japanese counterparts.

At the outbreak of the Pacific War, he was in Japan and was unable to return. He finally came back in 1955 with a one-year limited visa. Frank Wolverton recalls this anecdote for *Black Belt Magazine:* "After six months in Southern California he was invited by the Fresno Judo Club. In a very short time in Fresno he captured the love of his young students and the respect of the older students, many whom were professional people—judges, doctors, teachers and police officers. It wasn't long, though, before his visa ran out. The people of the area didn't want him to leave, but the visa regulations were definite. Such was the admiration of the people of Fresno for Yamauchi sensei that they presented a petition to Congressman B. F. Sisk, bearing the signatures of 600 men, women and children, asking him to bring a special bill before Congress to allow their judo teacher to stay. Sisk was in the process of taking the petition before the House of Representatives when Yamauchi received a telegram from the immigration authorities—his visa had been extended indefinitely."

Yamauchi's teaching was classical. He emphasized discipline and respect asking his students to accept only the best from themselves, never to allow themselves to give in to weakness: "If you hurt your leg, you still have another leg. Get up and run." "If you die tonight, learn something this morning." He liked to put the stress on the fundamentals of judo, stressing "kuzushi by rhythm motion." Next to judo Yamauchi collected rocks, and fishing was his favorite activity and favorite topic of discussion.

FROM JUJUTSU TO JUDO

Although many individuals and businesses harbored discriminatory attitudes toward the Japanese Americans, many did not. It was within this environment that the Japanese American communities experienced a cultural revival after the war and upon settling into their old or new communities. In early 1946, Buddhist temples and Shinto shrines began to function again as formerly interned priests returned from the camps. Japanese shops and stores opened once again, and many of them catered specifically to the Japanese community, not necessarily because they wanted to but more because they were the only ones who would utilize their services. With the renewal of the Buddhist temples and Shinto shrines came the revival of the Japanese activities and programs that were associated with them, including Japanese language schools, the women's associations, and cultural activities such as *obon* (worship of the ancestors) and New Year's functions.

Thus judo was part of the cultural revival and reaffirmation of the Japanese American communities. Many dojos along the West Coast, including the Seattle dojo and the Portland Obukan dojo, reopened. In fact, in the Los Angeles area, the Seinan dojo had kept its doors open throughout the war, with Jack Sergei as the instructor. During the war the members of the Seinan dojo actually visited the Manzanar internment camp in order to do judo with the internees to improve their judo skills. In doing so Sergei lost his job with the Los Angeles Police Department and later became an actor.

Judo also grew in other areas around the country, owing to the fact that many Japanese Americans settled in these areas after the camps. In 1950, George Kuramoto helped to start the Denver dojo, which became one of the most successful dojos in the country in the 1950s and 1960s. In 1950, the first judo club in Salt Lake City, Utah, was started by Frank Nishimura and George Akimoto. Also in 1950, Hank Ogawa helped to revive the Ontario Judo Club in Ontario, Oregon, which was later renamed the Ore-Ida Judo Club. In 1952, judo was begun in Caldwell, Idaho, by Mas Yamashita.

After the war the popularity of judo re-emerged. The four original *yudanshakai*—Seattle, Hawaii, Northern California (Hokka), and Southern California (Nanka)—all began operations again. They were soon to be joined by the emergence of a fifth *yudanshakai* in Chicago. In fact, Chicago was an area to enjoy the growth of judo after the war.

Vince Tamura had taught at the Jiu Jitsu Institute during the war in 1944. In 1946, judo was started at the Lawson

Courtesy of Fukusawa Akio

Ishikawa Takahiko with James Takemori, Donn Draeger, Kenzo Uyeno, and fellow judoka from Philadelphia.

YMCA by Hank Okamura, a longtime leader of organized judo in the Chicago area. The Chicago Yudanshakai was formed in 1947 with John Osako as its first president. The Chicago Yudanshakai also received a direct charter from the Kodokan, having the authority to promote individuals to *sandan*.

The period of time from the 1920s to 1950 was witness to great shifts in the Japanese American communities. These shifts can be captured by the dynamics between traditionalism *versus* modernity, assimilation *versus* accommodation, Japaneseness *versus* Americanism, and Issei *versus* Nisei. Emerging after the war the Nisei became leaders in the Japanese American communities, and this shift corresponded to a shift from a segregated Japanese immigrant settlers' community to an assimilated model community.

During this period of time, sports played a large role in the social fabric of the lives of the immigrant and Nisei families. While baseball, basketball, and volleyball could be understood and viewed as examples of assimilation and acceptance, judo was clearly a sign and symbol of cultural preservation and reaffirmation. The practice of judo in the camps reinforced its focus on education and self-defense, and minimized its perception as a sport or challenge-based entertainment. Contrary to kendo with its use of swords, judo has no stigma of Japanese nationalism. But it did offer the Japanese American communities a way to preserve their idealized notions of Japanese culture that they had brought with them from Meiji Japan. In short, judo itself had emerged from this time period with a different set of values, attitudes, and beliefs that were reinforced in its codes, rules, and sanctions. This view of judo not only laid the groundwork for the tremendous expansion of judo in the next two decades, but also provided the foundation for conflict in the future.

First National AAU judo championships, 1953. Standing: Joseph Knight; Aloysius C. Holtmann; Dominick Carollo; Samuel S. Luke; Robert W. Smith; Charles Yerkow; Kimura Mitsuho; Donn F. Draeger; (?); (Richard Yennie ?); Harry Kurisaki; (?); (?); Kenneth Kuniyuki. Seated: Doiguchi Suketaro; Henry Stone; Uchida Yoshihiro.

THE GROWTH OF JUDO

The creation of a governing body in the period just after World War II was a turning point in the history of judo in the U.S. Before World War II judo had developed cultural roots as a consequence of the commitment of Issei and Nisei leaders who favored Kano's educational goals. Initially, Issei teachers had reproduced in the U.S. the Japanese *ryu* or school system of their homeland. Thus, *yudanshakai* were traditionally regional organizations dealing directly with the Kodokan. With a national organization, that is, a national American authority, a new era was to come. Many of the changes that occurred have to be attributed to the combination of two main forces—on one hand, the dedication and expertise of the Japanese community judo teachers and, on the other hand, the growing role played by a newcomer in the U.S. judo microcosm, the armed forces of America. United in their efforts, they promoted Kodokan judo. However, the influence of the institutional, financial, and legal powers of official military structures was to redefine significantly and definitely the codes, finalities, and hierarchies in use during the first half of the 20th century.

Words are not without significance. The establishment of such an organization whose name changed from *Beikoku Judo Yudanshakai* to Amateur Judo Association, then to Judo Black Belt Federation of the United States of America and finally to United States Judo Federation in less than two decades raises numerous questions. The central one deals with the context that fostered the changing of structure from a local to a national basis and its impact on American judo. Successive titles reveal the evolution in process during the post-World War II period. The Japanese method of educating the minds and bodies progressively gave way to a westernized, multiethnic, and contest-oriented sport. Once dominant, the emphasis laid on the pursuit of character building came to be challenged by the quest for records.

Courtesy of Emilio Bruno

Henry Stone and Emilio Bruno.

Henry Stone established the JBBF Foundation for administrative purposes as well as the AAU Foundation for Sport Judo Competition.

PROMOTING KODOKAN JUDO

The years 1950–1952 stand out in the history of postwar judo. The groundwork for the many future changes and new developments was laid in those years. It was to spark off a renewed interest in judo and a chain reaction in which all the actors interacted. The relations between the U.S. and Japan began to improve as the Korean War started. Because of U.S. military interest in judo general interest grew in this era of conformity. Emilio Bruno was instrumental in formally renewing the contacts with the Kodokan that the war had officially destructed. Thanks to his friend Kotani, a meeting was arranged with President Kano Risei in 1950. New plans for American judo, which had been previously elaborated by Henry Stone and Kimura Mitsuho, were discussed. Henry Stone had painstakingly tried to establish a much needed national unity. The organization of judo as a national and international sport was a key issue in the letters he had regularly sent to the five existing *yudanshakai*.

First issue of the *Official Judo Bulletin* featuring Lyle Hunt, 1953 AAU Grand Champion.

In 1952, the judo leaders of the *yudanshakai* of Seattle, Hawaii, Northern California, Southern California, and Chicago formed the first U.S. national organization, the Beikoku Judo Yudanshakai under the leadership of Dr. Henry Stone. The representatives were: Doiguchi Suketaro and Kimura Mitsuho of Northern California; Nagano Kiro, Kuniyuki Kenneth, and Murakami Seigoro of Southern California; Harry Kurisaki of Hawaii; M. Miyazaki and George Wilson of Seattle; and Tamura Masato and Nagano Hikaru of Chicago. Donn Draeger of the U.S. Marine Corps and Emilio Bruno of the Strategic Air Command also contributed efficiently. During the first meeting held one year later, the name of the organization was changed to the Amateur Judo Association (AJA). The executive board of this new organization consisted of Dr. Henry Stone, president, William Godfrey, vice-president, and Uchida Yoshihiro, secretary-treasurer.

USJF Archives

USJF Archives

They were all elected to two-year terms. The composition of the board of governors tends to show the slowly evolving nature of American judo, the wish to go beyond factions, to reconstruct after World War II. Issei and Nisei judo leaders joined forces with representatives of the Army and university educators.

One of the major characteristics of the national AJA organization was that the authority to grant rank was assumed by it. High-ranking individuals were no longer permitted to grant promotions on their own and all the *yudanshakai* agreed to come under the umbrella of the AJA. This move was designed to ensure the uniform administration of rank standards across the country. In turn the AJA granted *yudanshakai* the privilege to promote through the rank of godan, 5th degree black belt, within themselves. All rank promotion applications higher than that, however, had to come before a national rank evaluation board and be approved there. This structure of rank governance still exists in the USJF today. In addition to the development of procedures for rank promotion, one of the first things the AJA did was create a Public Relations (PR) Committee whose job was to communicate with its members. This was part of the effort by the national organization to establish a communication network across the country. Thus from 1953, the AJA published a series of "Official Bulletins." Uchida Yoshihiro was chairman of the PR Committee, and one could see that the AJA also referred to itself as the "National Yudanshakai." In 1955, the AJA changed its name to the Judo Black Belt Federation (JBBF) of the U.S., and in 1963, "upon recommendation of the JBBF Executive Committee, the Board of Governors [has] unanimously adopted 'United States Judo Federation' as an additional name to be used by the Federation." Under the leadership of then president Kenzo Uyeno and then successor Fujimoto Hiro, the JBBF launched a national rank registration procedure coupled with a detailed rank identification system. This was the basis of the financial stability of the organization. The JBBF, which was renamed the United States Judo Federation in 1969, also adopted a new comprehensive constitution and

USJF Archives

Kenzo Uyeno.

Entrance of the
Kodokan decorated
on the occasion of
the first Japan–USA
meet, Tokyo, 1956.

by-laws, and established a national communication forum through their publication, *Judo Bulletin*. Since the beginning, dan ranking had been a key issue. However, it was not the only difficulty enthusiastic judo leaders had to face. An earnest effort was made to revise the constitution and by-laws. In a message published in March 1954, Henry Stone justified changes to the board of governors: "The proposed composition is one designed to give representation and a voice to all agencies which are actively and industriously promoting Kodokan Judo. This was effected in the earlier draft but was not outlined specifically." The links between the Kodokan Institute and American judo were so close that many of the Japanese standards, requirements, and procedures were in use in the United States.

A decisive step was made by Stone and Uchida with the agreement between the JBBF and the Amateur Athletic Union (AAU) in December 1952. The Amateur Athletic Union, formed in 1888, was a national organization for the promotion and encouragement of amateur sports and physical education throughout the United States. Judo was on the fringe of the world of institutionalized sport. The policy of inclusion developed by Stone and Uchida aimed at protecting judo identity and gaining a social legitimacy. On March 2, 1960, in a letter to Daniel J. Ferris of the AAU, Uchida Yoshihiro recalled the complexity of the

Courtesy of Jim Bregman

1956,
Washington
Judo Club.
Ishikawa sensei,
center, wearing
glasses.

situation: "It was with great difficulty on our part and with much reluctance that the judo members joined the AAU. Their one great fear was the AAU would dictate policy to the JBBF, once judo became established in the U.S.A. Both Mr. Stone and I used the argument that the AAU was a democratic organization and would abide by the decision of the largest group in the United States. Our purpose in joining the AAU was to help standardize judo in the U.S. through one system—the Kodokan system of judo—and to eliminate the many hybrid forms of judo that existed in our country at that time. Also, to run district championships and National championships annually for the AAU. The AAU was not to enter controversial matters such as giving out ranks in judo for the proficiency of individuals in the sport, but only to see that the contestants were amateurs in good standing."

In December 1952, during its annual meeting the U.S. AAU recognized the AJA as the sole grantee of judo rank in the U.S. and incorporated judo into its competitive sports program. According to the agreement: "The Judo Black Belt Federation of the U.S.A. recognizes the Amateur Athletic Union of the United States as the sole governing body of all amateur Judo contests and exhibitions conducted in the United States. [...] recognizes only those district and national championships sanctioned by the Amateur Athletic Union of the United States. [...] recognizes the responsibility of the Amateur Athletic Union for the participation of the U.S.A. in international Judo competition sanctioned by the International Judo Federation, by virtue of the Amateur Athletic Union's membership in the International Judo Federation, as the U.S.A. representative.

"The Amateur Athletic Union of the United States, by reason of the Judo Black Belt Federation's close association with the Japanese Judo Institute (Kodokan), recognizes the Judo Black Belt Federation as the sole

American judo was highly honored when James Bregman and Hayward Nishioka were asked to perform *nage no kata* during the 1963 All Japan Judo Championships in Tokyo.

Opening ceremony of the first international Japan–United States of America judo meet, Tokyo, 1956.

Courtesy of *Black Belt Magazine*

organization within the United States as qualified to make belt awards for proficiency in an understanding of Judo. [. . .] shall not recognize belt awards in Judo which are not sanctioned by the Judo Black Belt Federation. [. . .] agrees that the total responsibility for the procedures and conduct of all examinations held for the purpose of grading and for granting belt awards shall be vested with the Judo Black Belt Federation of the U.S.A."

This agreement was beneficial to the new judo organization because it placed judo under the umbrella of a recognized sports institution. In 1953, the First National Judo Championships was held with AAU sanction, and judo had apparently taken a long step toward becoming a national sport. The AAU was unanimously accepted as a member of the International Judo Federation. In exchange, however, the AAU agreed that the AJA was the only organization in the U.S. that could grant ranks. By doing so the JBBF retained its power in exercising authority over the development of judo in the country.

Thus in parallel development with the officers of the AJA came the establishment of the National AAU Judo Committee. This committee controlled all international competitions for U.S. amateur judoists. From 1963 the AAU and JBBF joined forces to publish, distribute, and sell joint handbooks (1963, 1964, 1966, 1968, and 1970). Sales of the books were handled mostly by the JBBF and exceeded 100,000 copies, owing to the large judo population at the time. All of the proceeds were given to the AAU Judo Committee to help finance its operation and development. From 1950 to the mid-1960s judo grew to become the third largest sport among all the sports under AAU jurisdiction.

JUDO IN THE ARMED FORCES

The relationship between the armed forces and the Japanese method of fighting dates back to the beginnings of the 20th century when the virtues of courage, teamwork, leadership, and loyalty were seen as natural components of sporting behavior, and consequently took a large part in the military training. Sports programs regularly involved football, wrestling, and self-defense. In the Army, sports were used as analogous

USJF Archives

General Curtis Emerson LeMay chose judo to buttress the fighting spirit of elite troops.

"It's amazing the effect Judo has both physically and psychologically. It's a tremendous builder of self-confidence. And you can get just as much exercise as you want."

to war, and wrestling was considered as the "nearest thing to actual war approached by man." Before the war, judo was one of the many hand-to-hand fighting techniques taught by Army wrestling instructors. Combat classes included tumbling, boxing, wrestling, disarming, and judo.

In *Kill or Get Killed*, an early WWII manual representing a "selection and combination of techniques taken from judo, wrestling and other body-contact sports," close-combat expert Colonel Rex Applegate declared: "through the centuries, unarmed combat tactics became more refined and skillful, until they reached their peak in the commando-type training given in certain of our military units during World War II." Efficiency was the main concern. On February 9, 1942, at the height of the Pearl Harbor hysteria, *Life Magazine*, a widely read weekly pictorial, showcased judo tricks with a political twist. It demonstrated to the average reader that Army judo, taught by an insider, loyal to America, was now part of close-combat techniques. Judo was used as an element of war propaganda. The "war secrets" of the enemy were to be reversed against them. Under a reassuring title, "Army Trainees Learn Jujitsu, Loyal U.S. Japs Teach Them," head instructor Shibukawa of Camp Roberts, Southern California, displayed some tricks "fairly easy to master" in order to meet the enemy on even terms: "Boy, now we'll give'em a dose of their own medicine!" Despite his contribution to the war effort, Akira Frank Shibukawa was relocated to Camp Robinson, Arkansas, in May 1942.

In *Martial Musings*, judo historian Robert W. Smith highlighted the difference between prewar and postwar military judo: "Marine Corps judo bore no resemblance to the sportive jacketed wrestling I encountered in Chicago after being discharged in 1946. Marine judo was a mélange of punches, chops, elbows, and low kicks—most of them aimed at the groin. No throws or locks, just strikes by the number. We were told that every Japanese private was a samurai who would eat two of us with his one bowl of rice and then hike fifty miles with a seventy-pound pack. So we had to out-terrorize them. We believed it."

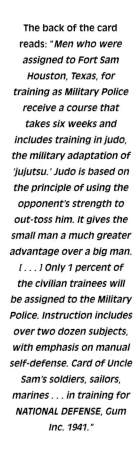

The back of the card reads: *"Men who were assigned to Fort Sam Houston, Texas, for training as Military Police receive a course that takes six weeks and includes training in judo, the military adaptation of 'jujutsu.' Judo is based on the principle of using the opponent's strength to out-toss him. It gives the small man a much greater advantage over a big man. [. . .] Only 1 percent of the civilian trainees will be assigned to the Military Police. Instruction includes over two dozen subjects, with emphasis on manual self-defense. Card of Uncle Sam's soldiers, sailors, marines . . . in training for NATIONAL DEFENSE, Gum Inc. 1941."*

USJF Archives

Curtis Emerson LeMay was the architect of U.S. strategic air power and the key engineer of modern judo in the Air Force. During the Cold War, the Strategic Air Command (SAC), which he led, became America's primary deterrent force. LeMay built it into a combat ready command. In 1950, he decided to launch an unprecedented judo program to allow combat crew members to face survival situations, "a valuable tool for the command's air police and security forces," "a means of self-defense for combat flyers who might someday be forced to bail out over enemy territory." LeMay thought that judo associated with other conditioning programs would keep crew members fit and alert during their long and difficult missions.

General Thomas S. Power was in charge of the implementation. To head the program, a top U.S. wrestler was chosen who happened to be the highest ranking Caucasian judoist, Emilio Mel Bruno. Bruno's contribution proved to be peerless because of his long-lasting friendship with Kotani and close Kodokan leaders. Bruno's introduction to judo came via wrestling. His foster father, Roy H. Pop Moore, had been taught wrestling by World Champion Frank Gotch. Following Pop's career, Hayward Nishioka wrote in *Black Belt Magazine:* "By this time, Pop Moore was gaining a strong reputation as top wrestling coach. His high school team kept beating every other YMCA and college team around including UCLA. Pop's successes were so impressive that Dr. Jigoro Kano personally asked him to coach the Japanese Olympic wrestling team. Two players gained international fame: Hatta Ichiro and Kotani Sumikichi." In 1935, shortly after the Olympics, Pop took the very first U.S. wrestling team to Japan. Emilio Bruno was a member of the American wrestling contingent. He developed a strong interest in judo as a consequence of a tour meant "to improve U.S.-Japanese relations and to promote the expansion of wrestling in Japan and judo in the United States."

In 1963, in the first *Official AAU Judo Handbook*, General Power, who was then SAC commander-in-chief, summed up his philosophy: "It has been my personal experience that judo is more

In 1953, the United States Air Force Strategic Air Command invited a group of Kodokan experts in judo, karatedo, and aikijutsu for the purpose of training Air Force personnel. Standing: Kobayashi (judo), Ishikawa (judo), Kotani (judo), Tomiki (aikido), Bruno. Kneeling: Nishiyama (karatedo), Obata (karatedo), Kamata (karatedo).

Courtesy of Emilio Bruno

Courtesy of Emilio Bruno

than just a sport or a means of self-defense. It builds courage, alertness and the ability both to exploit the opponent's weakness and to anticipate his moves. To engage in the sport of judo thus helps a man to gain not only confidence in his capabilities, but also a realistic evaluation of his limitations. As a result, he learns to accept any challenge without taking unnecessary risks. All these qualities are indispensable to the men of the Strategic Air Command if they are to discharge their vital and difficult duties effectively. It is for this reason that I have always endeavored to promote an active interest in judo among the men of SAC and to give them opportunity to become proficient in it."

The involvement of the Strategic Air Command in judo was due to the evolution of the political backdrop. During this period, military judo programs benefited obviously from the soaring military expenditures linked to the containment policy. The interest the Army had in judo took a new turn and spurred general attention. In Japan, judo also became part of foreign policy and Kodokan delegates received significant support from the Japanese government. At the end of 1951, Kodokan experts engaged in a world tour to promote Japanese judo and culture while future SAC teachers received instruction from the best Kodokan professors. In a report about judo in the SAC, Sergeant Charles Meredith declared: "The first class, a group of thirteen arrived in Japan, in 1952, and began learning Judo, Karate, Aikido, and Taihojutsu. [. . .] Today, less than ten years later, the Strategic Air Command has more than 160 Black Belts Judo instructors, among them such champions as George Harris (4th degree, *yo-dan*), Toshiyuki Seino (4th degree, *yo-dan*), and Lenwood Williams (3rd degree, *san-dan*). At each of the 80 bases in

In 1951, Bruno was selected by General Curtis LeMay to be supervisor of judo and combative measures at Strategic Air Command headquarters.

General Thomas S. Power and Emilio Bruno.

Courtesy of Emilio Bruno

Of all the goodwill tours of Japan, arguably the most memorable may have been the 1956 tour. The 22-man team arrived in Fukuoka on September 8, 1956, and the next day defeated a 9-man team of Fukuoka all-stars. They traveled to Tokyo by way of Osaka and Nagoya, competing in goodwill matches there, too, making their marks wherever they went. In Tokyo, they were welcomed with an impressive ceremony during which speeches were given by Kano Risei, head of Kodokan and then-president of the International Judo Federation; Major H. W. Blank, leader of the U.S. team; and Ryosuke Watase, managing editor of Mainichi Newspapers. In the competition against the top-flight Japanese all-stars, the Americans went ahead early in the *kohaku* (winner stays up) team tournament. The Japanese came from behind, however, to barely edge out the Americans. With 22 men on each team, Japan finished with only three men left. The matches were also attended by the U.S. Ambassador to Japan, John Allison, and the predominantly Japanese audience was reported to have given an enthusiastic round of applause for the American judo players.

The Growth of Judo

the United States and other countries where SAC men are stationed a full-scale Judo program is established. [. . .] The command's most important objective, though, preparing the combat crew members, has been achieved. More than 20,000 combat crew personnel have been trained in Judo's combative measures." Goodwill tours to Japan were organized on a regular basis to train judo instructors at the Kodokan.

Philip Porter, writing about the history of judo in the U.S., saw that period of intense development as decisive: "The SAC Judo Society was born in Omaha in 1954. Within a few years, General LeMay became Chief of Staff of the U.S. Air Force, and General Power went to the Air Research and Development Command (ARDC). The SAC Judo Society then changed its name into the SAC-ARDC Judo Society, and in 1959, at the first Air Force Championships the name was again changed to the Air Force Judo Association, with Phil Porter writing the constitution. The growth of this organization was so rapid that in 1961, it was necessary to change the name again to the Armed Forces Judo Association because Army, Navy and Marine Corps personnel were joining in large numbers. [. . .] The AFJA was at one time larger than all the black belt groups put together."

In November 1959, a judo instructor course was inaugurated at Stead Air Force Base, Nevada, at the SAC Land Survival School, which came to be considered as the "judo center" of the Air Force. Each course lasted five weeks, totaling 155 hours: judo, 36 hours; aikido, 12 hours; ka-

Courtesy of Emilio Bruno

Kotani Sumiyuki, Mel Bruno, Hosokawa Kusuo, and Pop Moore at Barksdale AFB, 1957.

Under wrestling champion Frank Gotch's expert instruction Pop became an excellent wrestler. When he was 17, in 1910, Pop recalls he competed for the World Wrestling Championship in Chicago against Mattie Matsuda: "I beat Mattie for the wrestling title, but he became my judo sensei." In 1935, in Tokyo, Kano honored Moore with a banquet for being the highest-ranking Caucasian judo black belt (second dan) in America. It was then that Moore, with the aid of his student Kimura Mitsuho, drafted the rules for international judo competition.

rate, 12 hours; air police techniques, 12 hours; air crew self-defense, 12 hours; judo tournament procedures, 18 hours; code of conduct, 5 hours; and training methods, 48 hours. Upon the completion of the course all trainees received the Air Force Certificate of Training and were awarded brown belts. Between 1959 and 1962, the 12 full-time instructors of Stead AFB's School of Judo graduated 10,000 students.

These impressive figures give a good understanding of the importance of the changes. In just a decade, the development of judo had reached unknown and unexpected levels. The minority of bizarre Caucasian people involved in the Japanese art had been turned into a mass of athletes not only skilled in the method of Kano but also in karatedo and aikido. But whereas Issei and Nisei sensei were, in cultural terms, judo-focused, Army coaches were sport and self-defense oriented. The Kodokan Institute was still considered the "Mecca of judo practitioners the globe over"; however, a new tendency had emerged.

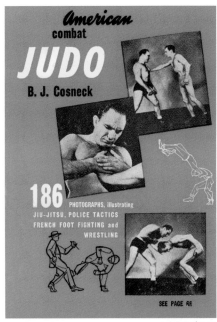

USJF Archives

American Combat Judo by Bernard J. Cosneck, 1959.

JUDO EXPANSION

With the establishment of a national board the 1950s were a period of growing enthusiasm for judo. A significant number of clubs were opened, some even outside any official structure. Richard Riehle remembers: "During the late 50's, as a teenager, I visited many of the dojos, including many of the unaffiliated dojos that proliferated throughout the middle Atlantic region of the East Coast. Much of my Judo was with those unaffiliated dojos, and many of the sensei who were originally trained in Japan." But most of them were gradually integrated into the USJF and new *yudanshakai* were created. Judo rapidly spread across the entire U.S.A.

USJF Archives

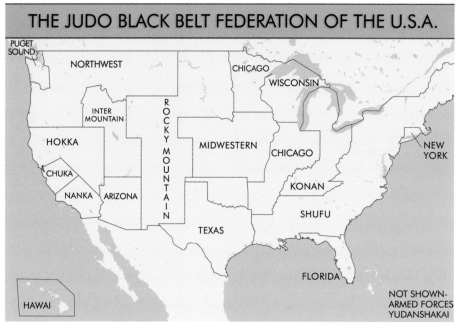

THE JUDO BLACK BELT FEDERATION OF THE U.S.A.

PUGET SOUND
NORTHWEST
CHICAGO
WISCONSIN
INTER MOUNTAIN
ROCKY MOUNTAIN
HOKKA
MIDWESTERN
CHICAGO
NEW YORK
CHUKA
NANKA
ARIZONA
KONAN
SHUFU
TEXAS
FLORIDA
NOT SHOWN- ARMED FORCES YUDANSHAKAI
HAWAI

Map of the Judo Black Belt Federation of the United States of America, 1962.

Map redesigned by Marion Brousse

New dojos in the San Diego area came under the jurisdiction of Nanka Yudanshakai under the invitation of Kenneth Kuniyuki. Sanshi Dojo in San Diego, taught by Matsubara Sachio, joined Nanka in 1955. Tsuji Benso, coming from Hawaii, became technical director of the San Diego Judo Club. In 1954, the Rocky Mountain Yudanshakai covered the states of Wyoming, New Mexico, Oklahoma, and Colorado. Only one dojo existed in Oklahoma in 1952. In 1962, there were enough black belt holders to join the JBBF as part of the Rocky Mountain Yudanshakai. In the mid-1950s, judo was started in Nebraska with Dr. Sachio Ashida at the University of Nebraska at Lincoln, and in 1961 the Midwestern Judo Yudanshakai was born, covering the greater part of six states (North and South Dakota, Nebraska, Iowa, Kansas, and the western half of Missouri).

The late 1950s and early 1960s saw *yudanshakai* in Arizona, Florida, Central California, Intermountain, New England, North Central (Wisconsin), and Texas. In New York, George Yoshida's senior students, including Ken Freeman, Joe Speyer, Eddie Basil, Hank Kraft, and Tony Pereira, organized the New York Yudanshakai in 1960. From its humble start with five *yudanshakai* in 1952, by 1963 the JBBF/USJF included 18; by the mid-1960s the USJF had an official registry of 20 around the country.

One of the oldest and largest *yudanshakai* was Shufu (Japanese for *capitol*), under the leadership of James Takemori. Shufu actually became a *yudanshakai* in 1953 and covered the entire east coast of the U.S. from Maine to Florida. It also included judo clubs in the Panama Canal Zone. Takemori, Kenzo Uyeno, and John Anderson traveled up and down the eastern sea-board to promote judo, giving clinics and holding examinations for rank promotions. Unlike the five charter *yudanshakai* of the USJF, the Shufu area did not have a large indigenous Japanese or Japanese American population from which to grow and form the basis of the judo world. A number of Japanese Americans did come to the East after the war, notably Dr. Koiwai Eichi, and there were a number who also were there prior to the war. But the Shufu area was mostly aided by judo people who came from the military, such as the imposing Donn Draeger.

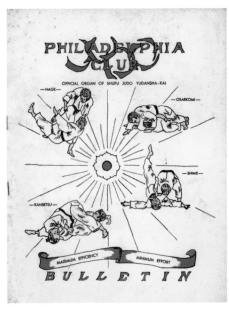

While most of the new *yudanshakai* were created for administration purposes, some were created out of the fact that existing ones became too big. The Chicago Yudanshakai, for example, originally had jurisdiction over Illinois, Indiana, Ohio, Michigan, Wisconsin, and Missouri. In 1958, dojos in Michigan were encouraged to form their own *yudanshakai*, and thus Konan Yudanshakai was created. It originally encompassed the states of Michigan, Ohio, Pennsylvania, West Virginia, and parts of Kentucky and New York. Even after this split Konan Yudanshakai included 75 dojos; the Chicago Yudanshakai included almost 3,000 members. The success of U.S. judo is translated into figures. In 1963, Philip Porter of the Air Force Academy and National AAU judo chairman recorded about 1,200 judo clubs in the country: 700 amateur clubs, 300 armed forces clubs, and about 200 college clubs. In addition, a large majority of YMCAs reported judo programs, none being counted in these figures. Although a precise evaluation of the total number of members proved to be difficult, Donald Pohl, secretary of the Judo Black Belt Federation, estimated the number of judo men at about 40,000, including approximately 1,600 registered American judo black belts. Such an evolution was made possible by a combination of social, organizational, and human factors.

Growth also meant adaptation to the evolution of American society and ways of life. The Detroit Judo Club (DJC) is a good example of the balance between traditions and modernity the followers of judo pioneers could preserve. Its history as it appeared in the January 1968 issue of *Judo Illustrated* reveals the dynamism of its members. "In 1952, the Detroit Judo Club consisted of 15 members meeting one night a week at the local YMCA. Fifteen years

Ishikawa Takahiko exemplifies the leading role Issei judo experts played in U.S. judo. In *Martial Musings*, Robert W. Smith recalled: "What a wonderful man and a fine judoka he was! After drawing with Masahiko Kimura in 1949, Ishikawa won the All-Japan honors in 1950. He taught judo to U.S. Air Force personnel in 1953 and, with Air Force patronage, moved to Philadelphia in 1955. There he taught judo and served as technical advisor for various U.S. judo organizations. In 1967, he moved to Virginia Beach, Virginia and opened his own school; and in 1984, at the age of sixty-seven, he became the youngest 9th dan in Kodokan history."

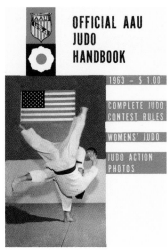

OFFICIAL AAU
JUDO
HANDBOOK

1963 ~ $ 1.00

COMPLETE JUDO
CONTEST RULES

WOMENS' JUDO

JUDO ACTION
PHOTOS

USJF Archives

later, the DJC was operating its own 10,000 square foot dojo. What transpired during those 15 years is an interesting story. The beginning of the club was not unlike that of hundreds of other clubs. A lone instructor introduced a basic course at a YMCA, a handful of students showed up, and the first course ended with some interest in advanced studies. It was at this time that Hiro Fujimoto decided to expand his idea by offering both beginning and advanced courses coupled with plans for the formation of a club. As the number of black belts increased, so did the classes, until judo was being offered at all of the nine Detroit metropolitan area's YMCAs.

"Although the club was headquartered at the Downtown YMCA, its activities rotated among the various Y branches to take advantage of each day of the week. So successful were the multi-Y classes and advertising program that the club soon outgrew YMCA facilities. Confronted with the increasing activities of other Y programs, the club was forced to move its operation out of the 'free' YMCA to a low-rent second-floor factory loft. The new home of the Detroit Judo Club, although less than desirable, was still home. The members took pride in ownership and collectively renovated the facilities. As each of the nine Detroit area Y classes graduated, students were invited to a club novice *shiai* and get-acquainted session.

"It was at this time that the club decided to take advantage of its annual *shiai* as a means of additional revenue. The first *shiai* had been held shortly after the formation of the club and the date, the first Saturday in June, had been picked more out of convenience than for timing. It was at this time that the policy changed. Every member would be given 10 tickets, which could not be returned. As an additional incentive, a list of attractive merchandise was offered for ticket sales in excess of the minimum 10. Prizes ranged from transistor radios and cameras to expense-paid trips to New York and Florida. All awards were valued at 40% of the ticket value, so the club realized a 60% profit on all sales over the minimum assessment. In addition to individual awards, a chance on a $500 savings bond was incorporated with the ticket to help melt sales resistance.

"John Osako, 6th dan, former Pan American and National AAU Grand Champion and head of the USJF Standards Committee, joined the Detroit Judo Club in 1961 and was head instructor for the club's 700 members. Osako's goal was to develop more well-rounded judokas, which accounts for the emphasis placed on refereeing, katas, terminology, and the other requirements of the sport. Like

"Of course I'm proud that you made Shodan. But please take it off until we get home!"

"Of course I'm proud that you made Shodan. But please take it off until we get home!"

most coaches, he pressed hard to develop champions but never at the expense of the well-rounded judoka. Osako took great pride in the caliber of his brown belt referees. Backing up the club's 400 junior members were the Parent Boosters, whose organization supervised junior activity, and raised money for out-of-town *shiais*. The Booster Club, patterned after Chicago's Uptown Dojo Boosters, held dances, sold hot dogs and soft drinks at the dojo, and did the clerical work of the club. All revenue derived from their activity went to the betterment of junior judo activity at the club. Hiro Fujimoto, 6th dan, USJF President, was the original founder and first president of the club but had since taken a back seat, preferring to entrust the operation of the club to what he liked to call the 'future leaders of U.S. Judo.'"

When asked about the phenomenal success of the Detroit Judo Club, Fujimoto declined to take any of the credit, praising "the smart men he keeps around him who deserve all the credit." Innovations developed by the DJC, and now incorporated on a national basis, included the national rank registration system, the color-coded *shiai* scoring card system, membership application folder, self-adhesive officials' badges, and many other administrative and technical aids. The rise of the Detroit Judo Club from a 15-member organization to the largest non-profit club in the country was more than a coincidence; it was the by-product of organization and hard work.

As Don Pohl, the club executive secretary for the past 15 years, remarked, "the Detroit success, if you want to call it that, was born out of hundreds of meetings and get togethers where everyone was encouraged to participate and contribute." Don Crane, the club's energetic president, felt that the future of judo hinged on the junior development program with immediate activity and support coming from the parents of the juniors. Given the proper leadership, Crane felt that the parents could take any given club and transform it overnight: "if you can interest the kids, you can sell the parents, and if you sell the parents on the value of judo your club is on the road to success." For some, judo became a family affair. Tamura Masato was often seen with daughter Diane on television shows in the Chicago area. In California, the Carollos showed the way with their two children. They offered an example of a close-knit judo-oriented family. The method of Kano was presented as the cornerstone of a satisfying life. As suburban America grew, "judo moms" certainly contributed to the development of judo by praising the activity.

OSAKO

John Osako.

Fight between John Osako and Michel Dupré by French judo cartoonist Claude Fradet'. Paris, December 1953.

97

Post-World War II judo benefited largely from America's reconversion to a peacetime economy and the subsequent evolution of society. The U.S. basking in the glory of having won the war experienced economic and social booms. Between 1945 and 1961, the U.S. gross national product more than doubled, and standards of living increased dramatically. The birth rate soared and continued to exceed over four million a year until 1964. The baby boom, coupled with postwar economic prosperity, meant continued business for builders, manufacturers, and school systems. Among important social changes was the concern for education. The baby boom became a grade-school boom. Parents were convinced that success in school was a prerequisite for success in life. Many GIs returning from the war took advantage of the Servicemen's Readjustment Act of 1944, the GI Bill of Rights, and enrolled in college. The law provided them with living allowances and tuition payments, and over one million GIs enrolled in 1946, about half of all college students at the time. The GI Bill was one of the many shock absorbers meant to cushion the economic impact of sudden demobilization. Some GIs who had had previous judo experience during their military services and the war taught judo in college.

"Must be one of those American GI's."
by Dave Enslow

Courtesy of the Kodokan Institute

Kano Shihan interviewed by NBC, 1936.

THE IMAGE OF JUDO IN POSTWAR AMERICA

The appeal of judo in postwar America is culturally significant. The mystique of traditional judo continued unabated for most judo connoisseurs. Even during the war, it lured some, like young Dick Yennie, who taught himself Japanese, became a translator for the War Department, a judo expert, and later held several offices in the Midwestern *yudanshakai*. As a rule, postwar judo had to be promoted in the country to be socially acceptable and to build up greater general support. The most significant factor in the changing image of judo was the growing influence of television and films. A combination of causes helped to give judo a multi-faceted image over the years. First, the image of judo had to be redefined in the minds of the general public and for some it had to be reconstructed because prejudice against the Japanese still lingered. The evolution of American society impacted the development of judo. One factor that directly influenced this growth was that the general public's perceptions of Japan and the Japanese were changing. Over time and quite rapidly, the Japanese recovered a positive social image. General MacArthur had planned for such changes to occur as part of the recovery of the country. During the Korean War anti-Japanese sentiment waned. Even though no other period can be compared to the days when Japan's feats of modernization and its triumph in the Russo-Japanese War had validated a whole way of life, a brief parallel could be drawn between the jujutsu craze that peaked in 1905 and the great interest taken in judo in the 1950s and the following decade.

In both cases, the activity was primarily spectacle-oriented. With swiftly changing technologies and the fantastic development of the media, judo gradually started to command larger audiences as leisure time increased. Promotional shows, fairs, army tournaments, and Boy Scout jamborees contributed to the Americanization of the image of judo. The weeklong Pan Pacific Sportsmen's Show in April 1953 featured judo with the help of the Tegners' National Judo Association. Bruce Tegner, a former California State Champion and U.S. armed forces instructor, his sister Carol, and six-year-old Van Norman appeared in their judo falling routine. This show, with 300,000 people visiting the venue, and the presence of actress Linda Darnell and Paul Hesse, a Hollywood photographer and a black belt holder, had all the characteristics of an all-American spectacle with KTTV News Reel taking pictures for the record.

"No, I don't agree with you there," corrected Craig, continuing his examination of the body. *"And yet it is not a case of drowning exactly, either."* *"Strangled?"* suggested O'Connor. *"By some jiu jitsu trick?"* I put in, mindful of the queer-acting Jap at Clendenin's. Kennedy shook his head.

The Dream Doctor, by Arthur B. Reeve, 1914.

USJF Archives

The Arthur Godfrey Show, 1954.

USJF Archives

Joe Weider's
"Trainer of the
Stars" Judo
Course, 1959.

Some elements that had boosted the trend, when judo had made its first entry into the popular consciousness, were still present. Mystery novels and films had abundantly fed collective representations. Over the years judo emerged as an alternative sport worthy of understanding on its own terms. TV transformed American uses of leisure as entertainment came to be regarded as a right fully integrated into the lives of Americans. TV became a crucial force in consumer culture. The average TV viewing time reached five hours a day in the mid-1950s and shaped the minds of generations of viewers. Actually, the links between the Japanese art and television had been concomitant to television's origins. John Logie Baird, the first to invent a mechanical system of television, came to New York in 1931. On October 18, he gave a speech at WMCA and WPCH radio stations about his impression on the city and his work on television. To explain the success of TV in England, he declared: "Television is now broadcast regularly through the British Broadcast Corporation, and our programs include such things as small plays, boxing matches, and jujitsu demonstrations." It took time before Baird's prophetic words turned real in the U.S. Jujutsu was part of the *Lum 'n Abner* radio show on September 8, 1941 (*Lum and Abner Practice Jujitsu Holds*). Beginning in the early 1950s, the exposure of judo on state (Tamura Masato, Chicago, February 10, 1950) and on national TV networks became part of the USJF promotional efforts. Kano's Chicago visit

*Lucille and Viv
Learn Judo,
February 25, 1963.*

received wide coverage. The popularity of the judo act by the Tamuras, father and daughter, attests to the complete turnabout that occurred in 1952. Interest for judo grew. It reached a peak in the late 1950s–early 1960s on the *Ed Sullivan Show* (August 5, 1956, *U.S. Air Force Talent Show*). It can be safely assumed that the publicity given to the Air Force program on the *Ed Sullivan Show* blurred animosity and convinced even the most reluctant who still harbored ill feelings toward their wartime enemy. The *Lucille Ball Show* (February 25, 1963, *Lucille and Viv Learn Judo*)

USJF Archives

illustrates the way family show producers exploited the humoristic facets of that new trend.
Television took judo out of the dojo and brought
it into the living room of the average American
family.

Movies and TV series contributed largely to
the promotion of judo. Being a black belt became
a symbol of human and social excellence. From
the start, TV provided both good and bad
publicity. George Wilson, who organized and
commentated a TV demonstration in 1953 on
the occasion of a collegiate ball game, certainly
knew what was needed to make more people
aware of judo. Some like Jeanette Bruce, a
novelist and a journalist for *Sports Illustrated,*
took to judo because of TV. Curiosity led her to
learn judo in Kanokogi's New York dojo. In the May 22,
1967, issue, in "Confessions of a Judo Roll-Out," she related
with humor her first grueling but exhilarating experience
on the mat: "All I knew about judo until a few weeks
ago was what I had seen on television—a demonstration
showing a couple of little girls (like me) throwing men
built like Anton Geesink right into the next studio."

On the screen, the stress was put on the spectacular
aspects of the Japanese art. Two main characters,
Charlie Chan and Mister Moto, were icons of the time.
Their ability to solve the most intricate cases was based
on Oriental wisdom and the mastery of hand-to-hand
combat. The stories of Charlie Chan by Earl Derr Briggs
and of Mister Moto by John Phillips Marquand quickly
appeared on the air and on the screen. Farkas and
Corcoran, who have been researching martial arts in the
movies, quote *The Outside Woman*, in 1921, as the first

Courtesy of *Black Belt Magazine*

**Sean Connery
received judo
and martial arts
instruction from
Donn Draeger for
the role he played
in *You Only Live
Twice*.**

**Dick Tracy and
Jo Jitsu.**

101

Judo Joe,
August
1953.

use of martial arts by the U.S. film industry, but they see postwar films as essentially different. "The modern era of eastern martial arts began in 1945, after World War II had introduced elements of Japanese culture to Americans at large. In *Blood in the Sun,* for the first time a Hollywood star, James Cagney, used Asian combative techniques, those of judo, to defeat an antagonist. His attempt to inform the West of the war pits him against the Tokyo chief of police for the climactic one-on-one battle." Besides opening a new era, *Blood in the Sun* exemplifies a different utilization of judo. The expertise was not on the Japanese side. It was even used against its originators, breaking ethnic barriers in order to place judo in the service of the values of courage and justice. Bruce Tegner was one of the influential people who introduced judo to Hollywood in the early 1950s. Through his *National Judo Association* school, he developed a personal approach and was frequently called on for technical advice and instruction of actors for spectacular fight scenes. "Judo goes to Hollywood" Tegner stated in 1953, in his magazine featuring famous actors like Groucho Marx, Bob Hope, Cornell Wilde, and many starlets and models learning the Japanese method.

Judomaster,
November 1965.

It may even have appeared for some to be an American takeover. Some films served as a vehicle for a new perspective. The jujutsu-judo mix was part of the arsenal of the loyal and the brave. The success of judo was advertised all over the world by a wide range of films that fed more dreams like *The Seven Samurai* by Akira Kurosawa (1954), *The Pink Panther* with Peter Sellers (1964), James Bond adventures like *Goldfinger* (1964) and *You Only Live Twice* (1967) with Sean Connery, or *The Green Berets* with John Wayne (1968). A long list includes television series like *Johnny Staccato* (1959–1960) with John Cassavettes, *The Avengers* (1964– 1969), *Honey West* (1965–1966), *The Green Hornet* (1966–1967), *The Wild, Wild West* (1965–1969), and others.

The image of judo was often exploited as a Cold War prop on the screen and as a source of comic relief. In the film version of Nabokov's *Lolita* (1962), judo was used as a sexual metaphor to spice up bland dialogue in a hotel lobby scene. It served to announce the linguistic games of the budding sexual revolution. Judo had clearly become so trendy that it was found everywhere. It revealed the media thirst for sensational events. But few spectators realized that judo proficiency came only from hard work, something Bruce Tegner had learned with Kuwashima Shozo.

Humorists and cartoonists were also part of the game. Numerous evidence could be given of heroes gifted in the art. Comic strips often centered on characters like *Judo Joe* (1953), *Judomaster* (1965), or Dick Tracy's crime busting pal Jo Jitsu (1960) or Judy Jitsu (1967) to mention only characters named after their skills. This shows how the various dimensions of the entertainment world had captured the Japanese art.

In the 1960s, judo was no longer a confidential activity restricted to the Japanese community or to a group of

Playboy Magazine,
January 1965.

"Nice defensive move,
Miss Mullins . . . !"

Reproduced by Special Permission of Playboy Magazine. Copyright 1966 by Playboy

"One kiss is worth two judo chops any time!"

connoisseurs. "One kiss is worth two judo chops any time!" Snoopy's philosophy as it appeared in the *Chicago Tribune* showed that the method of Kano had become a household name. In January 1965, on the back of the Playmate centerfold, in the main cartoon of *Playboy Magazine*, artist Sokol depicted a *randori* scene during which a yellow belt lady dodged the attack of her black belt opponent. The jacket went off and left her topless under the applause of her admirers: "Nice defensive move, Miss Mullins . . . !" The presence of judo in the nation's number one TV family show *I Love Lucy* in 1963, in *Playboy* two years later, and in a Snoopy comic strip in 1967 clearly shows the ubiquity of judo and its popularity in all walks of life. Judo had entered the middle class family circle. It was seen as sophisticated and exotic enough to be the focus of a men's magazine joke and entertaining enough to be part of kids' world. It had something for everyone.

Of course, the coverage and the publicity made about Kano's method did not bring knowledge about its real

Black Cat © Lorne-Harvey
Publications

**A judo lesson by
Black Cat.**

meaning. The gap remained between reality
and representations of reality. The popularity
of judo in American high schools was tested
by Olympian Ben Campbell. The author
publishing his results in the January 1971 issue
of *Judo Illustrated* qualified judo as "probably
the least understood sport practiced in
the United States today." He added: "the
objectives of Judo; i.e. self-control, discipline,
moral responsibility [...] have always seemed
far-fetched to those watching a rough and
tumble judo match." Figures showing that
"high school boys had a very limited, almost
nil, knowledge of what real Judo is" revealed
the difficulty for the method of Kano to gain
an identity and a status in American society.

In fact, the image of judo as a self-defense
method was so deeply anchored that the general public's
representation never failed to underscore spectacular
features. In the preface to the third edition of his book
Kill or Get Killed, Colonel Applegate gave some keys to
understand this phenomenon when he wrote: "The danger
of overrating judo as a means of combat lies not only in the
aura of mystery that has been allowed to surround it, but
also in the overemphasis placed on it as an effective means
of hand-to-hand combat training during World War II. As
a result of that war and a demand by the public for books
and methods on fighting, bookstores were flooded with
books and pamphlets on the subject of unarmed combat.
[...] Extravagant claims of success of the unarmed judo
exponent against an armed enemy are frequently made.

*Popular Science Magazine
logo and trademark used
with permission of
Time4 Media, Inc.*

[...] The illusion of ease in subduing an
opponent and the implication that this can
be accomplished without personal risk or
injury to the user, are also fallacies evident
in many instruction courses in close combat
offered to the public."

Despite efforts made in the field of
communications, the general public still had
a somewhat confused representation of the
Japanese method. The images of mystery
and invincibility existing at the beginning
of the 20th century were still vivid and
exploited for entertainment or marketing
purposes. However, by the mid-1960s it was
no longer enough to promote judo. In 1966,
Hayward Nishioka denounced the absence

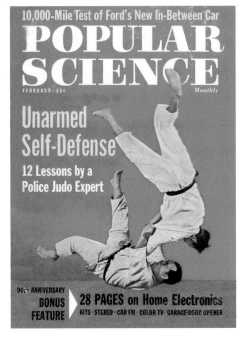

105

of visibility that characterized judo in the media. "Not one major newspaper in the U.S. covered the recent World championships in Brazil. This is disheartening to the players [. . .] Many people don't know what real judo is. All they are exposed to are television versions."

The image most judo leaders tried to support was somewhat different from the media-promoted version. Their aim was to encourage a wholesome Kodokan judo. This continued to be done on a regular basis in traditional dojo with the help of promotional tournaments featuring judos experts. As it was stated in the constitutions of all *yudanshakai,* dojos were meant to be non-profit corporations. Many wished to see this as a legacy of the samurai code. They rejected as a breach of judo decorum the publicity hype and its commercial side effects. They condemned the so-called "judo scavengers" in judo-karate contract schools who were engaged in the art for personal profits or those who associated with disreputable businessmen. In the mid-1960s, such individuals were identified and prosecuted or, in the case of non-U.S. citizens, extradited. But the specific ethical problems raised by commercial judo were still a constant cause of concern in the 1970s. The recurrent frauds used by the "conmen" who threatened "true judo" amply justify the reluctance of the judo leaders to adopt a different policy. Television marketing procedures, which today are the norm in most sports, were not accepted then in many circles. The issue of amateurism versus professionalism was still at the center of many rancorous debates. In the judo world most chose to follow the original code of ethics. Traditionalists could not tolerate any technical or moral transgression. Any display of the attractiveness of judo without the emphasis on morals and culture was seen as a sacrilege.

The impact of judo making its debut as an Olympic sport was not as strong as it could have been. Jim Bregman's bronze medal certainly gave an immense boost in prestige and stature to high-profile judokas in judo families but major newspapers failed to enthusiastically endorse the judo results. The tugs-of-war in some *yudanshakai,* the absence of financial backing, the growth of other sports that were more business-oriented, and the social and political context probably hampered the further diffusion of the image of judo at a time when it was most needed.

Bernard Pariset (France).

Lyle Hunt and Kawaishi Mikinosuke, 1953.

"Remember our motto . . . 'Use his weight to your advantage'."

THE SPORT OF JUDO

As art and sport, judo took a firmer stance in American society as a method likely to improve the lives of a large number of Americans. During that period, the method of Kano evolved with a shift from East to West, a transition from education to sport, and the emergence of a period of "bureaucratization" and "sportification." In two decades, judo became part of the Olympics and of the armed forces, was included in AAU tournaments and in collegiate sports associations, and consequently gained full credibility in the world of American sports. Due to the dedication of postwar leaders, judo was offered a strong organizational system and its future development was planned. With the AAU agreement, a national judo contest began to be held on a regular basis from 1953 onward. The first National AAU Championship took place in San Jose, California. There were four weight classes (–130 pounds, –150, –180, and heavyweight). The winners were Hatae Kenichi of Hawaii, Charles Nakashima, Don "Moon" Kikuchi, and Lyle Hunt, all of the Pacific AAU area. After matches between the winners of the individual categories, Lyle Hunt was awarded the overall grand champion title. The main teachings of the first national judo event were two-fold: weight categories had been introduced in judo contests, and a Caucasian had won the grand champion title. These two elements are vivid evidence of the westernization of judo in the U.S. Lyle Hunt, from San Jose State College, was recognized as a brilliant judo fighter. However, many traditionalists viewed weight classes as a moral transgression.

HUNT

Lyle Hunt.

Uchi mata by "Tosh" Toshiyuki Seino.

USJF Archives

Courtesy of the Kodokan Institute

Despite a general reluctance, judo contests with weight divisions were not a new issue. According to AAU wrestling historian, Don Sayenga: "the weight category system and the tournament rules were patterned from our Olympic wrestling tournament wrestling system. All this unfolded from an old copy of the first competitive judo rules and weight system developed by R. H. 'Pop' Moore Sr. at the request of Dr. Jigoro Kano during the 10th Olympic Games at Los Angeles in 1932. 'Pop' was Japan's first Olympic wrestling team coach. Dr. Kano envisioned the need for a weight system that far back, particularly, he was impressed with the conduct of the Olympic Wrestling competitions (scoring, rules, and weight categories, etc.)."

Similar influence can be traced back to Europe, where international judo matches with weight divisions were held as early as 1934, in Dresden, Germany. For non-Japanese coaches with a strong background of wrestling and physical education like Henry Stone and Mel Bruno, wrestling contests appeared as a model of organization. This explains the first proposal of weight classes (130, 150, 180, and unlimited) for judo matches made by Henry Stone and the Northern California judo technical committee in 1948. Besides the similarities between judo and wrestling, the adoption of weight classes was also due to political factors.

As a result of the occupation of Japan, at the end of 1945, the Supreme Commander of Allied Powers issued directives in order to put an end to the dissemination of militaristic and ultranationalistic ideology through martial arts practice. Subsequently, the Japanese Ministry of Education prohibited kendo, judo, karate, and naginata curricula in all schools, colleges, and universities. The *Dai Nihon Butoku Kai* and all military-related organizations were dissolved to dismantle the use of budo techniques for ideological purposes by a right-wing regime. Even though the Kodokan was kept open and Americans trained there after the war, it suffered from the political rerouting of Kano's ideals. In a letter dated February 28, 1948, Kawaishi reported to French Judo Federation President Paul Bonét-Maury: "Judo in Japan, now, have no control. Before war Kodo-Kan had a strong influence in Eastern part of Japan and Butoku-Kai controled a western part and they used give a Dan separately. All black belts aught to belong one of them, but it is changed now. Recently Butoku-Kai is no more exist and Kodo-Kan has half destroyed and no more influence. Each town in Japan has own organisation and gives Dan by their committee without old system. Some sections or Prefecturs formed a Judo Federation and controling few towns Judo organisations and give own Dan. Kodo-Kan may starts again and on the other hand a high graded Judo-Ka who belonged to Butoku-Kai may organise something, but there are so many Judo-Ka in all towns and they already built a strong influence." Even if biased, Kawaishi's analysis depicts the drastic consequences the ban on judo had in Japan.

However, the decisive move was made on the occasion of the inclusion of judo in the Olympic program. The path to the Olympics had been a long one. All through his life Kano devoted himself to the spreading of his method worldwide. Like Baron Pierre de Coubertin, he used the general interest in championships for the promotion of education and self-improvement through sport practice. Despite his interest in the wrestling tournament system, Kano had mixed feelings toward organized contests and the inclusion of judo in the Olympic program.

In a letter to Koizumi Gunji in 1936, Kano justified his hesitations and at the same time formulated a remarkable statement about the potentialities of judo and the traps implied: "I have been asked by people of various sections as to the wisdom and the possibility of judo being

Reinstatement of school judo, SCAP, September 13, 1950.

GENERAL HEADQUATERS
SUPREME COMMANDER FOR THE ALLIED POWERS
APO 500

AG 000.8 (13 May 50)CIE
SCAPIN 7265-A   13 September 1950

MEMORANDUM FOR: Japanese Government

SUBJECT: Reinstatement of School Judo

    1. Reference letter Ministry of Foreign Affairs, Chief of
Liaison Section, FOM No. 946 (EM), dated 13 May 1950, subject:
"Application for Restoration of School Judo."

    2. No objection is offered to the reinstatement of Judo in
the physical education and sports activities of all educational
institutions, as defined in the letter from the Minister of
Education, dated 12 May 1950, entitled "Request for Restoration
of School Judo."

    FOR THE SUPREME COMMANDER:

                                    K B Bush

                                K. B. BUSH
                            Brigadier General, USA
                               Adjutant General

USJF Archives

The first Pan-American judo championships were held in Havana, Cuba, on October 8–9, 1952. The Pan-American Judo Confederation was created on that occasion. Donn F. Draeger was elected vice-president.

introduced at the Olympic Games. My view on the matter, at present, is rather passive. If it be the desire of other member countries, I have no objection. But I do not feel inclined to take any initiative. For one thing, judo in reality is not a mere sport or game. I regard it as a principle of life, art and science. In fact, it is a means for personal cultural attainment. Only one of the forms of judo training, so-called randori can be classed as a form of sport.[...] The Olympic Games are so strongly flavoured with nationalism that it is possible to be influenced by it and to develop Contest Judo as a retrograde form as ju-jitsu was before the Kodokan was founded. Judo should be as free as art and science from external influences—political, national, racial, financial or any other organised interest. And all things connected with it should be directed to its ultimate object, the benefit of humanity. Human sacrifice is a matter of ancient history.

"Another point is the meaning of professionalism. With judo, we have no professionals in the same sense as other sports. No one is allowed to take part in public entertainment for personal gain. Teachers, certainly receive remuneration for their services but that it is in no way degrading.[...] Judo itself is held by us all in a position at the high altar. To reconcile this point of view with the Western idea is difficult. Success, or satisfactory result of joining the Olympic Games, would much depend on the degree of the understanding of judo by other participating nations." Twenty years later, the debate between the options "principle of life" and/or "sport" was marred by the ban on Japanese and German judo.

The controversy about weight classes was not restricted to the U.S. In Europe, experimental championships were held during the early 1950s. Postwar international judo leaders, like the Italian Aldo Torti, the first IJF president, and Edgar Schaefer from West Germany saw the future of judo in its inclusion in the Olympic program. When André J. Ertel was elected as head of the European Judo Union (EJU) in 1960, his first proposal was to have the weight class system definitely adopted (under 68 kg; under 80 kg; over 80 kg). Ertel recalled that "the EJU executive committee was perfectly aware that without weight categories, judo would not have the slightest chance of being accepted as an Olympic discipline. The Japanese Federation refused, at that time to consider weight categories." The final decision about the inclusion of judo in the Olympic Games

United States AAU Judo Grand Champion

1953
Lyle Hunt

1954
Gene LeBell

1955
Gene LeBell

1956
John Osako

1957
George Harris

1958
George Harris

1959
Lenwood Williams

1960
Imamura Haruo

1961
George Harris

1962
Shinohara Kazuo

1963
Shinohara Kazuo

1964
Uemura Gotaro

1965
Hayward Nishioka

1966
Eguchi Motohiko

1967
Nagatoshi Yasuhiko

1968
Watanabe Mitsuhoshi

1969
Noguchi Taizo

1970
Allen Coage

1971
Doug Nelson

1972
Douglas Graham

1973
Roy Sukimoto

1974
Irwin Cohen

1975
Tommy Martin

1976
Patrick Burris

program was taken in Rome on August 22, 1960. The 58th IOC session recognized the IJF as an Olympic International Federation, and judo was included in the program of the Tokyo Olympic Games by 32 votes to 2. Paul Bonét-Maury and André Ertel were the main architects. The 1964 Olympic championships with the victory of Dutchman Anton Geesink gave a new start to judo for at least two reasons. First, as an Olympic sport, judo gained a new identity in the world of modern sports. Second, by awarding the most valued title to a non-Japanese athlete, judo proved its international dimension.

U.S. JUDO CONTESTS AND CHAMPIONS

T he early years of the national AAU championships allowed non-U.S. citizens to compete. For that reason many of the competitors and subsequent winners of weight categories were Japanese citizens from Japan, such as the Uemura twin brothers, Gotaro and Kenjiro, the winners of the 1964 National AAU Championships in New York and former stars of Keio University. Other non-U.S. citizens also competed, such as Lhofei Shiozawa, the Brazilian national champion; Alan Petherbridge of Wales; and Doug Rogers, the Canadian national champion. This fact made the stellar performances of American judoists such as Kikuchi, LeBell, Harris, Nishioka, Campbell, and many others all the more spectacular. They clearly were on par with many of the best in the world. The national championships helped solidify that position and provided for the further growth of judo in the country.

Harris' story is a fascinating one. Born in Philadelphia in a residential neighborhood Harris started to learn boxing. Being talented he was tempted to become a professional boxer. However, after graduation he was drafted into the armed forces and sent to medic training at Travis Air Force Base in 1953 at the age of 21. During his stay in Texas he discovered racial discrimination and judo. He was introduced to a fighting

Prime Minister Ikeda Hayato met George Harris during his visit to Travis AFB, June 1961.

USJF Archives

method he had never heard of, by one of his patients who happened to be Phil Porter. Only two short years later, he placed third at nationals behind Osako. That same year he was chosen to compete on a tour of Japan with an American team composed of Osako, Ed Maley, Harold Sharp, and Gene LeBell. Harris finished the tour with a record of 21 wins and four draws. For five consecutive years (1955–1960), Harris won the Air Force (SAC) Championships. In addition,

in 1956, he twice won the gold medal at the Pan American Games, and took fifth at the World Judo Championships in Tokyo (1958) and in Paris (1961). He competed for the U.S. at the 1964 Olympics with Paul Maruyama, Jim Bregman, and Ben Nighthorse Campbell. Being a judo champion in those days was very demanding. Questioned by Rebecca Barnett about the sacrifices needed to become an Olympian, George Harris recalled: "I retired at a lower rank due to the constant judo travel and training demands. I missed out on promotions. I used to regret my slower advancement and lower rank than my peers. But I had to decide—what was my priority? It was to travel, train and focus on the Olympics. It made me a better person, gave me insight on life and people. Now, I would not trade those experiences for any amount of money." Rules were strict: "Rebecca Barnett: For a time you were a television celebrity? Harris: Yes, I appeared on talk shows and was twice a guest on *To Tell the Truth*. But as an amateur athlete I could not violate my status by accepting any money."

The abnegation of judo athletes was a routine occurrence in postwar judo. The individuals of the group composed by Lyle Hunt, John Osako, Donn Draeger, and Uchida Yoshihiro who participated in the 1953 Pan American team tour in Europe had to bear the costs of the trip themselves. Lyle Hunt was supported by the Lyle Hunt Citizens Committee of Alameda, California. Activities like all-star baseball game, putting contest, acrobatic dancing, twirling baton, and judo exhibitions reached a total of $1,100.

The 1960s saw other great judo players emerge as grand champions. In the 1962 championships in Chicago, a young Shinohara Kazuo of Los Angeles overwhelmed his opponents with his lightning-fast tsuri komi goshi, defeated Yoshida Shintaro and then Imamura Haruo, and won the grand championships. He repeated that feat in 1963 in Fresno, California. At the 1965 San Francisco

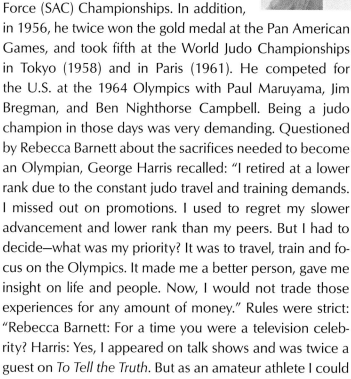

Ben Campbell, camp director, and U.S. team member Bill Paul with Professor Kotani at 1967 Camp Bushido.

A Graphic Novel of George Harris, by Victory Comics.

"Day after day, George and his fellow students were confronted with their own limitations. Each day they had to stretch farther, reach deeper into themselves to find a little more strength to continue. Not to give up, not to give in to the ever present temptation of just collapsing! They forced their bodies to yield to their will, watched closely by their unpretentious teachers who were so polite in their impossible demands."

nationals, a 165-pound Hayward Nishioka of Los Angeles won the grand championship. Nishioka won the Nationals again in 1966 and 1970 and in 1967 was Pan American Games Champion. In 1965 and 1967, he took two 5th places at the world championships

Tournaments conducted by the various branches of the armed forces also played a major role in the development of judo in the country. Like their counterparts in the civilian world, competitions provided enlisted men with new goals and objectives in their practice of judo. The first SAC judo tournament was held on April 7–8, 1954, at Offutt Air Force Base, Nebraska. There were both individual and team championships, and among the officials were General Thomas Power, Mel Bruno, Kotani Sumiyuki, and Otaki Tadao. These championships continued for many years, owing to the great popularity of judo in the armed forces. In time, other branches of the military held tournaments to further the growth of judo. One of the most memorable of these was the All-Marine Corps Judo Championships. These started in 1958 with four weight categories—under 140, under 160, under 180, and unlimited. At the National AAU championships, an overall champion was also crowned. For three consecutive years starting in 1959 a young marine named Ernie Cates, who was stationed at Parris Island, won not only the 180-pound division but also the overall grand championship, earning the distinction of being the top judo player in the Marines for several years.

Through this system of competition and training, SAC and armed forces personnel consistently emerged as some of the finest judo players in the country. In addition to Harris, Lenwood Williams of the USAF won the heavyweight and grand championships in the National AAU tournament in 1959. Seino Toshiyuki emerged in the early 1960s to become one of the best lightweights this country

Kodokan banner offered by Kano Risei, 1954, Offutt AFB. From left to right, Otaki Tadao, General Curtis LeMay, coach Walter Todd, overall champion M.A. Curtis, and Kotani Sumiyuki.

USJF Archives

has produced. In 1958, the SAC Judo Team was designated as the U.S. team competing in the Pan American championships, with Harris winning a gold medal, Mede a silver, and Reid a bronze.

Another proof of the vitality of U.S. judo was given by the constant interest in college judo. Henry Stone, previously introduced to judo in Honolulu's YMCA, in 1923 promoted the activity as a young University of California wrestling coach. College judo developed in the 1930s mostly in California with the help of Stone at U.C. Berkeley and Bruno and Uchida at San Jose State. World War II interrupted all collegiate judo. In the 1950s, a number of collegiate tournaments were held on the Pacific Coast quickly followed by Florida, the Southwest, the Midwest, New England, and other places. In 1962, the first national collegiate judo tournament was held at the Air Force Academy in Colorado. The same year, a survey on American college judo was compiled by Robert Wells, a New York City journalist and President of the Eastern College Association, and Major Philip Porter, Secretary of the National Collegiate Judo Association. One hundred twenty-two colleges were listed. Some were prestigious like Dartmouth, MIT, Harvard, Yale, Princeton, San Jose, Purdue, Cornell, and Berkeley, and others were less celebrated, but according to the authors of the report: "Every college that offers credit for Judo or Ju-Jitsu has found that the Judo section is always the first section filled." Wells concluded: "Making college judo a sport is one of the most important steps in making judo a truly national American sport."

Many elite athletes who competed as college students stressed the importance judo had for them as a mental discipline. The ability to stay mentally focused on the mat

"Another Bushnell student—I presume!"

First judo tournament in the armed forces, at Offutt AFB in Omaha, Nebraska, 1954.

USJF Archives

often goes with scholastic achievement and success in life. In 1992, Yosh Uchida was once again recognized for his sustained efforts in bringing judo to the collegiate scene.

The system of judo tournaments was also meant to encourage technically good judo. As a rule a player was eliminated when he had accumulated enough black points, usually five. For the first 20 years, competition was held using what was known as the "black point" system. Black points were earned according to the following procedure: victory by ippon: 0 black points; victory by decision: 1 black point; defeat by decision: 2 black points; defeat by ippon: 3 black points. Players were placed in a round robin format where they started competing against each other. As competition continued players would get knocked out because of black points. The players who remained after all had competed were the winners, in order of least number of black points to most. Players did not compete against each other twice. It was a grueling system and quite different from today's repechage system. Essentially, victories by ippon were necessary not to accumulate black points. Many players competing in large divisions actually were eliminated because they won five matches but not by ippon. The last time this system was used was the 1973 senior national championships in Atlanta. Today tournaments organized and conducted by the International Judo Federation utilize the double repechage system, in which players are placed into traditional championship-type blocks. Players who continue to win matches come through quarter-, semi-, and final round matches. Players who lose to the semi-finalists are then put into a losers' bracket (the repechage) and compete against each other to determine a repechage finalist, who competes with the losers of the semi-finals to determine third place. The final match determines first and second. This is the system in place today at the world championships, Olympic Games, and the senior national championships conducted in the United States.

On the world scene the 1950s saw the emergence of the first and second world judo championships in 1956 and 1958, both of which were held in Tokyo, Japan.

50¢

Black Belt

VOL. I, NO. 1   THE MAGAZINE OF SELF-DEFENSE

● JUDO ● KARATE ● AIKIDO ● KENDO

SPECIAL JUDO ISSUE
Complete National AAU Finals

Courtesy of *Black Belt Magazine*

Black Belt Magazine,
volume 1, number 1.

Representing the U.S. in the first world championships were Kimura Mitsuho and Vince Tamura. Tamura beat Chen from China by decision, Schlatter from Switzerland by ippon, but lost against Geesink. Kimura lost by decision against Courtine from France. In 1958, George Harris defeated Essink from the Netherlands, Cheng from China, and Yamamoto from Brazil, but lost against Sone. Ed Mede beat Mendoza from Brazil, but lost against Bloss from Germany.

In 1961 in Paris, Harris beat de Loureiro from Portugal, Zeiniawa from Poland, and Ehler from West Germany, but lost against Koga from Japan. Alseika lost his first match against Petherbridge from Great Britain.

The period from 1950 to the late 1960s was also significant. Seventy of America's top young judo men competed at the Olympic trials at the New York World's Fair in June 1964 to fight for the four spots on the U.S. Olympic Judo Team and the trip to Japan for the Olympic Games in October. On Friday, June 12, college student Paul Maruyama of Los Angeles took first place in the lightweight division (below 149.5 pounds), and AAU champion Jim Bregman of Arlington took the middleweight division (149.5 to 176.5 pounds). The next day George Harris won the heavyweight berth (above 176.5 pounds) and Ben Campbell of California took first in the open weight division. Alternates were Lloyd Migita, Harry Kimura, Bill Paul, and Dick Walters.

The success of postwar U.S. judo was recognized when Salt Lake City was designated as host city of the 5th World Championships. During the World Championships in Rio de Janeiro in 1965, Paul Bonét-Maury, general-secretary of the IJF, had approached Dr. E. Koiwai, chairman of the National AAU Judo Committee, and H. Fujimoto, president of the USJF, about the possibility of the United States hosting the 1967 World Championships. Bonét-Maury had followed the growth and progress of judo in the U.S. and thought that after Japan twice, France, and Brazil, it was time for the United States. Olympics for Utah, Inc., which had lost its bid for the 1972 Winter Olympic Games due to lack of experience in hosting an international event, showed interest in supporting the world judo meet. Finally, a solution was found to save money, and the final bid of Salt Lake City was accepted by the IJF. The World Championships were scheduled for August 9–12, one week after the Pan-American Games in Winnipeg, Canada.

Junior judo followed college judo. In 1964, the USJF and the AAU actively promoted a "junior division" with Charles Brown as Junior Development Chairman. The first junior nationals in Tampa, Florida, were attended with enthusiasm by 222 players from 14 states and Canada. The second junior nationals, held in Chicago, had an increased participation.

LESSONS FROM MY SENSEI

By Richard Riehle

As a teenager living in a relatively small Pennsylvania Dutch community during the mid 1950's, my experience of people unlike those of my community was limited. My ancestors were Old Order Amish . . . I discovered Japanese Martial Arts in our school library. E. J. Harrison's, The Fighting Spirit of Japan, *had survived the purging of the high-school library collection. Few in our town knew about Japanese culture except veterans and many seemed uninterested in martial arts. Some of my relatives found my fascination both alarming and disgusting.*

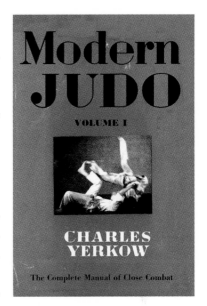

It was difficult to find a martial arts instructor during the 1950's. I began a correspondence with author Charles Yerkow. He helped me find and contact some Judo instructors in Baltimore, Washington, New York City, and Philadelphia. It was something of an adventure for a sixteen-year-old boy. I had to travel by bus, by train and then on foot to each city. From Mr. Yerkow I learned of a Judo demonstration to be held at Albright College in Reading, Pennsylvania. There, I met Jim Troutman, Donn Draeger, and Jim Takemori and I heard about the Washington and Baltimore Judo clubs. Troutman was my first real Sensei. He had earned his Shodan in Japan while a member of the U.S. Marine Corps. I was fortunate that he took the time to teach me the deeper philosophical values at the basis of judo.

I have particularly fond memories of Uyeno Sensei. He was the first to teach me how to eat with chopsticks. He understood the notion of personal centering. That was another major turning point in my life. Judo became a kind of mental activity, much like a fast moving game of chess, and later became a kind of meditative process. He was different from anyone this young Pennsylvania Dutch boy had ever known. His own family, U.S. citizens, had suffered during the War. Through him, and the others in his Baltimore dojo, I managed to gain a deeper understanding of Judo and myself in a complex world. The Sensei at the Washington Judo Club and elsewhere also guided me. Major Donn Draeger, USMC, befriended me and taught me new skills. After graduating from high school, I joined the U.S. Air Force, which had a spirited Judo program in the 1950's.

I stand now on the threshold of my eighth decade of life, in the dojo where I now teach and train. I am the old man with white hair. The lessons I learned from my early Sensei and from others like Ishikawa and Fujitani are as important to an old man, perhaps more, than they were to the young man from farm country trying to make sense of his life. I hope that my legacy will be a small fraction of that left to me by those who have enriched my life with their wisdom, their patience, their often justified impatience, their concern for my progress, and, ultimately, their friendship.

1964 U.S. Judo Olympic team. George Harris, Jim Bregman, Uchida Yoshihiro, Paul Maruyama, and Ben Campbell. As American minorities were asking for more rights the Olympian team prided itself on being an illustration of multi-cultural America.

NEW TRENDS

The changes that occurred in American society appeared to have been mirrored in judo organizations. In spite of two decades of continuous and sustained growth as the numbers of people practicing judo soared, strife and disagreements began to emerge. The reasons to be invoked in order to explain the fragmentation of the initial unity are of different origins. The evolution of U.S. mores and ways of life changed the tone and texture of social life. It necessitated continuous adjustments that judo leaders could not or did not want to make. The conflicts between individuals and interest groups, ethnic oppositions, the divergences in opinion upon judo finalities, and development policies were the main causes. The success of judo was based upon the ability of its promoters to give the method of Kano an identity and a solid embedding into the U.S. sport culture. Among the general public, judo specificity as a means of educating the youth was not only recognized but also much sought after and adopted. For all its internal differences American judo seemed to be on the path of becoming "an enduring American institution." The general public was being educated in the values and procedures of judo. High standards of conduct and performances could be maintained. Commitments far outweighed the particulars. But, the end of consensus came to disrupt the dynamic implemented by pioneers.

Chicago Judo Black Belt Association leadership, circa 1960. Back row: Neil Rosenburg, Dr. Paul Harper, Jim Colgan, Bill Kaufman, Okamoto Kenji. Front row: Phyllis Harper, Tamura Masato, Nagao Hikaru, Sam Maeda. T. Miyazaki, Hank Okamura.

Courtesy of Sakai Yoshitaro

FRACTURES IN AMERICAN JUDO

As in every human activity, tensions in American judo are part of its history. For long, fractions and infighting had occurred among the Japanese Americans themselves. But, rivalries between judo teachers or regional *yudanshakai* had always been controlled by the superior leadership of Kano and later by the Kodokan Institute. With the untimely passing of Henry Stone in 1956 a series of events began to occur on the national level causing a rift in the cooperation between the AAU and the JBBF. When Joseph Knight was nominated as AAU judo chairman his lack of recognition as a judo expert antagonized the vast majority of JBBF leaders. A campaign was started to remove Knight from his position and to have a real "judo man" selected. For that purpose, President Fujimoto circulated a memo stressing how U.S. judo culture and traditions were not taken into account in the AAU plans. He denounced the actions of "impersonating a black belt," the "usurpation of black belt rank," the attempts to "break bond with the Kodokan," and the desire to "establish a separate AAU ranking system." The policy of the AAU judo chairman hinged on options of "bureaucratization" and "Americanization," which the JBBF strongly criticized. The U.S. judo leaders did not want their practice to be considered to be a competition-oriented sport, and most of all they did not envision any form of independence from the Kodokan. In December 1961, Major Phil Porter was finally nominated as chairman. The next year, the Kodokan approved the new rank guidelines requirements submitted by the JBBF. The rifts between the AAU and the JBBF/USJF became even larger when the issues of amateurism and sanctioning touched off heated debates. Soon, with judo being the third largest sport in the AAU, there developed an open disagreement over philosophies, priorities, and control.

IJF meeting in Tokyo, November 1962. Standing: Hirota (Japan), Kawamura (Japan), Suk (Korea), Hatashita (Canada), Porter (USA), Hayakawa (Japan). Seated: Nauwaelerts de Age (Netherlands), Kano (Japan), Bonét-Maury (France), Delforge (Belgium), Ertel (France).

Strained relationships between the JBBF and military judo were another source of tensions. The SAC Judo Society, which changed into the Armed Forces Judo Association (AFJA), was admitted to the JBBF in 1955. But, in contrast with other *yudanshakai* limited by regional boundaries, the AFJA operated as a non-geographical association. The number of its members was disproportionally high. So was its technical influence with the programs implemented by the SAC in coordination with the Kodokan. Jurisdictional and economic problems were soon raised. Part of the monies from the members of the JBBF/USJF was sent back to each *yudanshakai* by the national body. The JBBF/USJF rule was to equally distribute the total amount to all the member *yudanshakai* at the time. Thus, even though the AFJA collectively comprised about one-third of the total membership base, it received only about 1/20th of the total pot. In addition, the AFJA had its number of votes in the Board of Governors and the Board of Examiners restricted to no more than the next larger *yudanshakai* in the organization.

Two other main issues enlarged the gap. Since the early days the question of whether the AFJA could or should admit civilians into its structure had been discussed. The JBBF/USJF had decided to allow civilians to join the AFJA. However, in 1966, the USJF moved to restrict the AFJA membership to civilian members, and continued to recruit military personnel as USJF members. This change was an attempt to curb the expansion, and thus the power, of the AFJA. Regardless of this decision the armed forces judo clubs continued to accept civilian and non-civilian members alike. Besides the military-civilian membership issue, the USJF dan ranking policy was at the center of the complaints. In June 1970, in *Black Belt Magazine*, Jim Bregman, then USJA Executive Committee member, made clear the secessionists' point of view: "Judo rank should be kept as a reward in fighting and coaching. [...] We don't attach community position to judo rank.

1963 AAU National Championships in Fresno. Ben Campbell, Obayashi Makoto, and Shinohara Kazuo.

USJF Archives

Courtesy of Jim Bregman

Uchi mata, by Jim Bregman.

"Most of us are in judo for the fighting and coaching activities involved rather than the social prestige, if indeed there is any in our American communities." Without innuendo Bregman attacked: "Judo rank giving has been abused because it has been used as a controlling device. The 'If you don't do what I say, you'll never get promoted' attitude is what we have seen too much of." Dan ranking problems are not specific to the U.S. They have always been a subject of discord in all the countries of the judo world. In France, for instance, during the same period the strict and conservative leadership of Kawaishi led to a schism that lasted for 17 years between the French Judo Federation and the National Black Belt College, and sequels have not vanished. The dan ranking issue is bound to cause a volatile political situation when it is linked to the struggle for supremacy of some groups or individuals.

In the particular case of the United States, this phenomenon was increased by a shift in judo mentalities and finalities as a result of the social evolution that occurred from the mid-1960s to the mid-1970s. In 1964, during the U.C. Berkeley Free Speech Movement, student activists suddenly contested the role of authorities on campus together with the leadership class in politics and the military in general. The campus crisis fueled dissent in America and led to a chain reaction. The civil rights struggle gained momentum. Feminists marched to combat male domination. Other minority groups also fighting for their rights demanded more visibility and the end of social exploitation. Hierarchical systems were questioned as the Vietnam War escalated and anti-war rallies multiplied. The status quo was regularly challenged and those who claimed to exercise absolute power were publicly condemned. Activists campaigned against the draft and attacked ROTC units on campus. Americans saw a breakdown in the sym-bols of power. The credibility gap widened. At no earlier time in history had the gulf between generations seemed so wide. In judo, traditionalists brought up in the seito-sensei or student-teacher chain of command suffered from this social evolution. As one sign of the changes, those who did not fear to behave like autocrats were openly criticized by a new generation of competitors who loved judo, had proved their skills on the mat, but denied any age-based scale of authority. The growing tensions between the AFJA and USJF continued to mount until AFJA leaders made the bold decision to break away from the USJF. At the same time there were some in the USJF who wished to disband or dissolve the AFJA. In 1969, the AFJA members officially withdrew from the USJF and formed the United States Judo Association (USJA). The 1970s were a dark time for American judo. This period is characterized basically by antagonism, name-calling, and discriminatory practices on all sides.

Underlying the supposed jurisdictional and economic problems between the AFJA and the USJF were strikingly strong cultural problems. On the one hand were the Japanese American Nisei, the old-guard leadership of the USJF. Having lived through the immigrant and internment camp experience, the only Japanese culture they knew of was very conservative, perhaps ultra-conservative, traditional, and rigid. Within that cultural framework they saw judo as a uniquely Japanese activity, and stood fast by their beliefs, at times rigidly, to protect the almost mythical cultural aspects of judo, such as the teacher-student relationship. There was an underlying air of superiority, captured in the sentiment that one has to be Japanese in order to be truly good at judo. Not only judo practice but organized judo was a totally Japanese thing. Even national meetings were held in the Japanese language, and Americans who attended and did not speak the lingo had to rely on the good graces of someone to translate for them. On the other hand were the armed forces personnel in judo. Mainly white, but sometimes not, they were decidedly Americans at heart who had learned to love the Japanese art of judo as their own. They had different mannerisms, personalities, and styles of communication that were inherently at odds with the traditional Japanese Nisei. They seemed more progressive, reform–conscious. They engaged their Japanese American counterparts as equals.

The Japanese American Nisei leadership were conservative while the white American leaders expected changes. The Nisei were content with the status quo, letting the general public find their way to judo, while the armed forces personnel wanted to be more active in marketing judo and recruiting members. For most Americans, it was

TOKYO 1964.

© IOC/Olympic Museum Collection

JBBF Teacher's Institute. Meeting with top technical and administrative leaders in Detroit, 1965. From left to right, starting at rear: Fujimoto Hiro, Frank Hubbard, Nagao Hikaru, Ishikawa Takahiko, George Uchida, Takamatsu Tooru, John Osako, Ashida Sachio, Charles Brown, George Wilson, Kitayama Hiro, Nakabayashi Sadaki, Tashima Shigeo, Vince Tamura, James Takemori, Donald Pohl.

Photograph by David Finch

**Ann Marie Burns,
first U.S. judo
Women's World
champion, 1984.**

not only admitted but also preferable for a student to ask a question of his teacher; for the Japanese American Nisei that was a challenge of the teacher, a violation of established dogmas. Aside from the distribution of monies, which was perceived by the AFJA as unfair, many AFJA members suffered from discrimination in questions of rank promotion. The Nisei leaders of the USJF kept a closely guarded hand on the committees that deliberated over rank promotions. For right or wrong, sanctions were placed on people through the withholding of rank promotions. The AFJA came to believe that they were unduly and strongly discriminated against in this area.

When the AFJA broke off from the USJF to form the USJA, the USJF still had in place its agreement with the AAU. It meant the USJF was the sole organization in the country whose ranks were officially recognized inside and outside the country. This was not a matter of no consequence since the AAU was the body that represented the U.S. in international affairs to the Pan American Judo Union and International Judo Federation. This fact was a major disadvantage to the early USJA, who wanted to compete on a par with the USJF. In the early 1970s, in fact, major battles occurred between the two organizations with regard to rank, with many in the USJF suggesting that the USJA rank was not proper or official. To remedy this situation the USJA finally sued in court for the right to issue its own ranks and for those ranks to be recognized, and in 1978 it won its court battle. This was a momentous occasion for the USJA and for the history of American judo in general, because that move basically sealed the fate of the existence of multiple national judo organizations in the country. Stereotyping, biased reactions, and discriminatory practices were recurrent not only in American society in general, but in the judo organizations as well. At the root of these powerful divisions were values of reformism versus traditionalism, rigidity versus openness. The microcosm of the national judo movement was disturbed by the ripple effect of the conflict that rocked the country as a whole.

The internal problems of the U.S. judo world were reflected on the mat as well. Despite the strong and prom-ising performances of American judo athletes in World and Olympic competition in the 1960s, the 1970s saw Americans slipping in their results on the international level. The judo World championships were held in Ludwigshafen in 1971, in Lausanne in 1973, in Vienna in 1975, and in Paris in 1979. In spite of their qualities, Americans fighters were unable to bring home a medal in any of these championships.

**Open Division
Champion**

1977
Otaka Shuichi

1978
Ishibashi Michinori

1979
Shawn Gibbons

1980
Dewey Mitchell

1981
Mitchell Santa Maria

1982
Mitchell Santa Maria

1983
Dewey Mitchell

1984
Michael Mika

1985
James Thompson

1986
Damon Keeve

1987
Damon Keeve

1988
Leo White

1989
Damon Keeve

1990
Damon Keeve

1991
James Walker

1992
Christophe Leninger

1993
Andrew Ruggiero

1994
James Bacon

1995
Kelly Rasnic

1996
Bryan Leninger

1997
Martin Boonzaayer

Of course, one major reason why performances suffered was the amazing rise in the competitive abilities of many countries around the world, particularly those from Europe. Spurred on by the Olympic and World championship performances of Dutchman Anton Geesink, judo in Europe skyrocketed in its popularity. Fellow Dutchman Willem Ruska also helped to kindle the judo passion in Europe with his gold medal at the 1967 Salt Lake City World championships. Still, one cannot help but wonder about the degree to which fractures within American judo contributed to the downward spiral of American results on the world level. Capacity was never an issue; stars such as Pat Burris, Irwin Cohen, Steve Cohen, Teimoc Johnston Ono, Tommy Masterson, and Tommy Martin had more than enough talent, spirit, and technique to be superb judo players. One of the brightest spots for American judo in the world scene, and the one exception to the American barrier to world medals, was provided by Allen Coage. Born in New York City, Coage was the national heavyweight judo champion in 1966, 1968, 1969, 1970, and 1975, and he took the grand championship in 1970. He was the first American judo player to win gold medals in two consecutive Pan American Games—the first in 1967 in Winnipeg, Canada, and the second in 1975 in Mexico City. He also won the Pan American Judo Championships in 1968 and competed in the World championships four times in 1967, 1969, 1971, and 1975, tying for fourth in the open weight class in 1971. He won the bronze medal in the 1976 Montreal Olympic Games.

REBUILDING AMERICAN JUDO

While the country reeled from almost two decades of social unrest followed by the Vietnam withdrawal, Watergate, and the Iran hostage crisis, the 1980s saw a newfound resurgence of conservatism. A new era of American judo dawned in 1978 when Washington legislators passed into law a federal statute (Federal Law 95-606) referred to as the Amateur Sports Act (ASA). The Act was designed to promote and coordinate amateur athletic activities in the United States. The United States Olympic Committee (USOC) was designated as the central coordinating agency for all sports on the programs for the Olympic and Pan American Games. Individual sports came to be controlled by national governing bodies that

Bob Berland, silver medalist, Seoul Olympic Games, 1988.

Photograph by David Finch

Photograph by David Finch

**Mike Swain, first
U.S. male World
champion, in 1987,
in Essen.**

were established with the USOC as states actors. In that particular case it meant judo was no longer ruled by the AAU but by a new structure, United States Judo, Inc. (USJI). The existing membership of the National AAU Judo Subcommittee was accepted as the membership of the USJI. The first president of the USJI was Frank Fullerton, who would remain in that position for 16 years.

American judo was restructured because of the formation of the USJI. The USJF and USJA became Group A members. They kept their internal structures and activities after 1980. Both were allowed to grant rank, receive and process memberships, and host their own tournaments, clinics, and other judo events. In addition state organizations were formed to become Group B members. Other national organizations, such as the Marine Judo Association and the National Collegiate Judo Association, became Group C members. In addition the current USJI structure includes 20% representation by athletes in all board, committee, and subcommittee affairs, and members at large. Under the new organizational framework, national championships and other national and international judo events, which are used as partial criteria for selection of United States teams in events like the Senior and Junior World Championships, the Pan American Games, and the Olympic Games, are organized by the USJI. Criteria for the selection of Pan American, World, and Olympic teams are developed by USJI and approved by the U.S. Olympic Committee, and subsequently these teams are selected to represent the United States in international competition.

In the 1980s, American judo experienced what was perhaps its best decade of performance in international competition. This was partly due to the pulling together of competitive judo under the umbrella of the USJI. This change occurred under the leadership of a new USJF president, Kim Wey Seng, a Korean-born U.S. citizen. Except for Henry Stone, all the presidents of U.S. judo had been of Japanese descent. In those days, Korean judo had proved its quality on the international level. It can be assumed that the choice of Kim as president appeared as a will for change expressed in some sort of continuity. This way, U.S. judo's Asian cultural background could be preserved, but sport results were expected. The influence of Korean judo was rather new. Actually, it is to be linked to their massive immigration to the U.S. In fact, Korean immigration started in the early 1900s but was limited until the 1965 Immigration

A splendid *tomoe nage* by Kevin Asano against Hosokawa Shinji from Japan.

Photograph by David Finch

Act when their community became one of the fastest growing Asian groups in the country. Soon Korean judo experts started to open clubs and to develop college judo. The U.S. judo world was a new scene of rivalry. The election of Kim Wey Seng in 1978 and his re-election in 1980 were evidence of the success Koreans could rapidly reach. The Korean influence declined with the re-election of Uchida in 1982, but still existed until 1988 with Kim Jong Oon as vice-president. The Korean episode of the 1980s announced the changes that were to occur at the turn of the 21st century with the arrival of new communities of immigrants, each of them bringing a different judo heritage.

America's first Women's World Champion was Ann Marie Burns (Rousey), who captured the gold medal in the under 56 kg division of the 1984 Women's World Judo Championships in Vienna, Austria. America's first men's World champion was Mike Swain. Mike Swain defeated Japan's Koga Toshihiko on his way to meeting and defeating Marc Alexandre of France in the finals. Mike Swain has the distinction of being one of the few individuals in the world, and the only American, to be in the finals of the World championships three consecutive times (in 1985 in Seoul, in 1987 in Essen, and in 1989 in Belgrade). Other American athletes brought distinction and honor to American judo through their medal performances at the World championships, including Kevin Asano, Lynne Roethke, Margaret Castro-Gomez, Darlene Anaya, Bob Berland, Eve Aronoff, Dewey Mitchell, Christine Pennick, and Mary Lewis. Youngsters Joey Wanag and Jason Morris brought back medals from the 1983 and 1986 World championships for juniors (under 20 years of age) in Puerto Rico and Italy, respectively.

Americans excelled on the mat in Olympic competitions. Eddie Liddie and Bob Berland brought home bronze and silver medals, respectively, from the 1984 Olympic Games before hometown crowds in Los Angeles. Kevin Asano defeated 1984 Olympic gold medalist Hosokawa Shinji of Japan in the semifinals only to narrowly lose to Kim Jae Yup of South Korea in the finals of the 1988 Seoul Olympics, taking a silver medal. Swain brought back a bronze medal from that same Olympics.

The 1980s were also significant for the U.S. on the international organizational scene. Under the leadership of Rusty Kanokogi, one of the pioneers of women's judo not only in the U.S. but also the world,

Photograph by David Finch

Leo White.
At the 1984 Olympic Games, Leo White defeated the leading champion, Robert Van de Walle, Belgium. In 1992, in Barcelona, he repeated his feat, beating Stéphane Traineau from France.

Photograph by Bob Willingham

Hillary Wolf, 1994 junior World champion. Hillary Wolf is also a well-known movie star. She played the role of Megan McCallister, Macaulay Culkin's sister, in *Home Alone* and *Home Alone II*.

the U.S. was host to the first women's World judo championships in New York City in 1980. A World championship for women was then successively held in Paris, 1982, Vienna, 1984, and Maastricht, 1986. Since 1987, the women's World championship event was combined with the men's championship, and these two championships have been held together every two years ever since. The Los Angeles Olympic Games also brought Olympic judo to the U.S. for the first time. At the same time as the USJI turned its attention to judo on the international scene, the USJF and USJA looked inward and focused on their own issues and concerns.

After the formation of the USJI, the USJF came back under the leadership of the Japanese American Nisei, many of whom had been the same people who had formed the USJF in the 1950s and had led it through the 1960s. With them the traditional mentality of Meiji Japan returned. Uchida Yoshihiro was once again elected president of the USJF from 1984 to 1988, as competing powers were operated behind the scenes in the names of Kimura Mitsuho of San Francisco and Kenneth Kuniyuki of Los Angeles. The latter saw their resurgence in the mid-1980s as "gaining back the seat of power of the USJF that had been usurped by a strong Korean influence." With Uchida, Kimura, and Kuniyuki, and the emergence of the USJI to handle international affairs, the USJF reverted to many of its old ways. It had no development program per se, except the giving back of registration monies to the *yudanshakai*, a program that was in place 30 years before. With its ability to grant rank promotions, the USJF leadership seemed content with the status quo.

Unfortunately, this newfound ultracon-servatism resulted in a decreasing number of USJF members in the 1980s to an all-time low of around 4,000 members in 1988. This figure is in stark contrast to the 100,000 judo participants in the 1960s. Moreover, the re-gaining of power by many of the same leaders of American judo some 40 years earlier meant that there was a great and deep void in the development of leadership. Many of the third- and fourth-generation Japanese Americans were conspicuously absent among the talent

Jason Morris.

Courtesy of Jason Morris

pools that the organizations could tap for leadership positions. Radically different, the USJA appeared as the reverse image of the USJF. Where the USJF was conservative with its rank granting, the USJA, under the leadership of Phil Porter, appeared to begin handing out rank left and right in exchange for memberships and donations. Whereas the USJF did no marketing of judo, the USJA engaged in an active campaign to raise money, mainly to create a national judo center near the U.S. Olympic Training Center in Colorado Springs, with the express purpose of placing as many USJA members on the national squad as possible. Whereas the USJF was unable to develop judo in the country, the USJA during these years appeared to have gone too far in the exact opposite direction, selling judo and allegedly giving ranks to the highest bidders. None of these organizations succeeded in their programs. The USJF was left with dwindling numbers, and the USJA was left in dire financial straits. While the creation of the USJI was intended originally to provide a means by which the two parties could come together, instead what seemed to occur was a return to rigid, almost defiant ideologies and values on the part of all three groups.

Photograph by Bob Willingham

Brian Olson captured the bronze medal in the 1997 World Championships in Paris.

The American Judo of the 1990s

The structural changes that cropped up in American judo due to the Amateur Sports Act and the formation of the USJI meant that rebuilding judo in the dojos and local areas came to be the field of action of the two national organizations, the USJF and the USJA. In fact, while there has been some disagreement about the purview of the organizational structure of judo in the U.S., the ASA indicates strongly that the USJI concerns itself exclusively and directly in international matters with regard to competition and training.

All other questions of judo development in the country, therefore, would rightly fall within the purview of the USJF and USJA. The USJF responded to its all-time low in membership in 1988 by electing a slate of officers who would embody the traditional values of Kodokan judo but who would adopt a more progressive stand on judo development in the country. These ideals were embodied by

Bob Berland, Mike Swain, Kevin Asano, Eddie Liddie, Jason Morris, Jim Bregman, and Allen Coage united against drugs.

Photograph by Bob Willingham

**Jimmy Pedro,
World champion
and two-time
Olympic medalist.**

Yonezuka Yoshisada of New Jersey, the newly elected president, and Robert Brink of Alaska, the new first vice-president. One of the first things the new executive board of the USJF did was to appoint David Matsumoto as Executive Secretary in 1989, in order to help re-organize and revitalize the organization, and implement the policies of the organization. Through a grassroots campaign of information dissemination and major restructuring and personnel shuffling of its key committees, the USJF then began the slow process of rebuilding.

A major step in this process was the election in 1992 of Robert Brink as the president of the USJF. Brink was the first non-Asian American president of the USJF since its beginnings in 1952. Under Brink's leadership the position of the Executive Secretary was converted to the position of Executive Director in 1992, and the USJF thus became the first judo organization in the U.S. to create such a position. A national office was formed with a paid staff under the supervision of the Executive Director, who was a volunteer at the time. Together with a new cabinet and the work of its first Executive Director, the USJF grew rapidly, climbing from its all-time low in 1988 to triple that to approximately 12,000 members in just six years in 1994. In 1994, the position of the Executive Director was converted to a paid one, and in 1996 the national office was moved to its current location in Ontario, Oregon.

The enormous growth in the popularity of the USJF Jr. and Youth National Championships was indicative of the resurgence in growth of the USJF during this time. At this championship in Hilo, Hawaii, in 1989, a total of 489 judo players competed. In 1995 in Los Angeles, and in 1996 in Oakland, however, the number of competitors at this same championship approached 1,000. It has remained close to this figure ever since. At the same time leaders in the USJA came to grips with many of the problems that had faced them when the USJA ran amok in the 1980s with promotion and financial problems. While the USJF saw a leadership change occur by the retiring of many key old-time Japanese American Nisei, the USJA saw a similar change occur when Philip Porter was retired from the presidency. The new officers, led by president Jesse Jones, then began the painful process of getting a handle on its promotion procedures and debt. After years of concerted effort by a determined board and membership, the USJA came out of the woods in the late 1990s to be once again a viable organization for the development of judo on the grassroots level.

American judo on the international and world level came under the supervision of the USJI. A new breed of competitors emerged on the world scene to bring back world and/or Olympic medals. These included Jason Morris' silver at the 1992 Barcelona Olympics, and his bronze at the 1993 World championships in Hamilton, Canada. Additionally, Jimmy Pedro won a bronze medal at the 1991 World championships in Barcelona, while Joey Wanag and Liliko Ogasawara both won silver medals at the 1991 and 1993 World championships, respectively. But many of these athletes' superb performances came more because of their own, individual sheer determination and hard work rather than through the aid of their sponsoring National Governing Body (NGB).

Part of the decline in competitive performance for American athletes in the early 1990s came from a sluggish USJI structure and function, and poor leadership in the areas of coaching and training. Despite the fact that the ASA was originally passed in 1978, it took 20 years for the USJI to reach an efficient organizational level. In January 1997, after witnessing the success of the rejuvenated USJF, the USJI hired its first paid Executive Director, who opened an interim National Office in a private office building in Colorado Springs, Colorado. In May 1997, a permanent National Office was opened at the U.S. Olympic Training Center

131

Complex in Colorado Springs, Colorado. In 1998, the USJI Board of Directors adopted the name USA Judo for the organization to bring it in line with the name of the governing bodies of most other sports (USA Basketball, USA Wrestling, and so on).

Thus in the latter half of the 1990s, with a new structure and new leadership in coaching and training, American athletes once again proved their competitive prowess in international competition. In 1994, in Cairo, Egypt, the U.S. crowned its first junior World champion, Hillary Wolf. Wolf is also known for her work as an actress and her roles in the *Home Alone* movie series. Liliko Ogasawara took a bronze medal at the 1995 World championships in Makuhari, Japan. Brian Olson came out of nowhere to take a bronze medal in the 1997 World championships in Paris, France. Sayaka Matsumoto won a silver medal at the 2000 World championships for juniors in Nabeul, Tunisia, the second highest place finish for an American (next to Wolf's win in 1994) in U.S. judo history. But the latter half of the 1990s belonged to one athlete—Jimmy Pedro. He won a bronze medal at the 1995 World championships in Japan. He then took a bronze medal at the 1996 Olympics before a packed, partisan crowd in Atlanta. After that he became unstoppable. Unfortunately, because of an injury he was forced to sit out of the 1997 World championships despite being the favorite to win his division. He came back with a vengeance in 1999, however, to win the World championships in Birmingham, England, defeating a tough Sebastian Pereira from Brazil in the semi-finals and Vitali Makarov of Russia in the finals. With that feat Pedro became the first American in 12 years to win the coveted World championships. At the time he won, he had amassed an amazing record of 81 wins and only 3 losses since the 1996 Atlanta Olympics.

While Pedro was clearly the star of the latter half of the 1990s, American competitive judo as a whole made remarkable progress. In 2000, for the first time American athletes had to qualify their weight categories in order to have the privilege to compete at the Olympic Games. The qualifications involved winning in competition primarily within the Pan American Judo Union. Americans responded; the U.S.'s standing in the Pan American Union went from #8 in 1995 to #2 in 1999. In 1999, American athletes stood on the medal podium an unprecedented 124 times (not including performances at the U.S. Open). Finally, in 2000, the U.S. was one of only four countries to qualify a full team—a competitor in every weight category—for the

USJF Presidents

1952–1954
Dr. Henry Stone

1954–1956
Kenneth K. Kuniyuki

1956–1958
Harry Kurasaki

1958–1960
Masato Tamura

1960–1962
Yoshihiro Uchida

1962–1964
Kenzo Uyeno

1964–1968
Hiro Fujimoto

1968–1978
Dr. Eichi K. Koiwai

1978–1982
Wey Seng Kim

1982–1988
Yoshihiro Uchida

1988–1992
Yoshisada Yonezuka

1992–1996
Robert C. Brink, Esq.

1996–2000
Mitchell T. Palacio

2000–present
Noboru Saito

Sydney Olympics, the other three countries to achieve this feat being France, Cuba, and Japan. At the Sydney Olympics, the U.S. Olympians won more matches as a team than in the past 20 years of competition; in so doing they defeated three 1999 World champions.

NEW INFLUENCES

The face of the U.S. today has changed considerably over the past decades. One of the most significant social phenomenon of our time is immigration. The world as a whole, and U.S. society in particular, has become increasingly borderless, and we are witnessing today the single largest tide of population movements in history. There are an estimated 130 million migrants worldwide, of which 30 million reside in the United States alone. In the past, the U.S. was metaphorically referred to as the "melting pot." This idea suggests that immigrants to the U.S. assimilate into an American culture, adopting the values, attitudes, and ways of life of American society. Theodore Roosevelt, in a speech before the Knights of Columbus in New York on October 12, 1915, expressed the idea as follows: "There is no room in this country for hyphenated Americanism . . . The only absolutely certain way of bringing this nation to ruin, of preventing all possibility of its continuing to be a nation at all, would be to permit it to become a tangle of squabbling nationalities." Yet most social scientists today

President Noboru Saito refereeing the final match between Lee Won Hee, Korea, and Vitali Makarov, Russia, during the Athens Olympic Games.

Photograph by Bob Willingham

would agree that the melting pot metaphor is not entirely accurate. American society today is less a melting pot than it is a salad bowl, a collective mixture of people from many different cultures. While people's original values were melted away in the melting pot, in the salad bowl they remain intact. They interact with people's ways from many other cultures to create a unique and interesting taste sensation.

Contemporary American society is in fact more like a kaleidoscope or mosaic and could have a strong social influence on American judo in the coming years. Today's American judo has been subjected to many different influences. Many parts of the country are still heavily influenced by the Japanese ways, especially in those areas with high concentrations of Japanese Americans (the West Coast, Hawaii, New York). Training methods, attitudes, and ways of thinking are all rooted not only in Japanese training methods but also Japanese customs and culture, and these influences continue to be strong. At the same time, the strong rise in popularity and competitive ability of many Europeans has influenced American judo strongly in many ways. European training methods, attitudes, and practices are willingly put into practice by many American judo teachers. In addition, as with their counterparts around the world, American judo leaders tend to look to France as a model for the development of judo in the country organizationwise. France boasts over half a million participants registered in their national judo federation, the result of a strong and concerted effort at marketing the educational values of judo in local communities. There are many other influences as well. Immigrants from Russia, for instance, living in New York, Philadelphia, and other areas of the U.S. bring their own style and brand of judo to their dojos. Immigrants and their descendant families from Turkey and Armenia have also emerged to be a force in American judo. And, greater interest in and appreciation of sport science methods and principles have allowed many dojos and their instructors to bring science-based training applications into their judo curricula across the country, especially in terms of strength, conditioning, and nutrition.

Consequently, it spawned a whole new breed of practitioners and different approaches. Judo today can be recreational, a method for achieving affiliation for children, adults, or their families. Judo can be a form of exercise and physical conditioning, as the nation's interest in health and exercise has increased. Judo can be a form of self-defense, as people around the country learn to defend or protect themselves in these times of great uncertainty. Of course

Ronda Rousey,
2004 Junior World
Champion, in
Budapest, Hungary.

Photograph by Bob Willingham

judo can be a sport, and many people around the country see judo primarily as one. The game of judo is a great one, and like all games carries its own adventure, fun, and excitement. And, judo can be a way of life. The goals and philosophies of judo since its original inception in the late 1880s can be used as a basis for self-improvement, social exchange, and social contribution. The intellectual, moral, and physical educational motives and goals of judo are ones that transcend time and space in history, and promise to be as important in the future as they have been in the past.

We live in a capitalistic world and our society is essentially a consumer-oriented society. Corporate culture has already adopted some of Kano's principles. Judo, therefore, should also be understood today as a consumer product. In order to be more successful in a highly competitive world in which the place of sports keeps growing, judo players, beginners or experts, need to be ambassadors of judo and find ways of bringing more and more people to adopt judo as a way of life.

When Kano created judo, he took into consideration the deep changes that were occurring in Meiji Japan. He transformed past Oriental martial techniques, integrating Western methodology and scientific approaches in function for the needs of a modern society. As a principle, adaptation to the social context proves to be a key to the understanding of the origins of judo in Japan. The success of French judo is directly linked to such a conception. Kawaishi used to say: "Judo is like corn or rice, it must be adapted to its soil." In this perspective, it might be said that judo has to correspond to the mentalities and times, to the culture and economy of the host country.

Since 2000, under the leadership of Noboru Saito, the USJF has actively and strongly pursued the development

Photograph by Bob Willingham

of judo through a process of strategic planning. This
process involves the analysis of the product we bring to
bear—judo—and the needs of the individuals and societies
in which they live. Based on such an analysis, the USJF
approaches the development of judo around the country
from a strategically conceptualized business plan. This
approach is strongly rooted in the scientific principles of
organizational development, change, and growth. This
transformation of organizational priorities, structures, and
functions is, as it always has been, a sign of the times,
and can be best understood from a social analysis of
contemporary American culture and society. The USJF is
the only organization of judo in America today that has
engaged in this process, and because of it the future of
judo in the country is once again bright. This business
strategy is a necessary move and should not be seen as
contradictory. It is needed in today's world. It does not
negate the amazing value of judo as a principle of life, an
art, and a sport.

JUDO FOR WOMEN

The history of U.S. women's judo is largely unrecorded
and would deserve a detailed study. Their gains on
the mat and their own persistence made it easier to
fight entrenched prejudices. They are now welcome in the
international judo community as fighters and referees. The
awards they receive often compensate for the fluctuating
number of medals obtained by male competitors. The
emergence and appeal of the Japanese method among
women often correspond to their struggle for autonomy

while the rich past of the land is mirrored in the lives of the pioneers. In the early days, during the jujutsu vogue the main concern of the advocates of physical culture was to fight the view of the physically limited female. Their publications were responsible for the upsurge of interest in self-defense for women. Imitating the women who in samurai families studied jujutsu for self-defense, an exclusive group of Washington high-society ladies took lessons from Yamashita Fude then from her husband.

At the height of the suffrage movement, self-defense seemed to be recognized as an implicit right. But unlike British suffragettes who studied jujutsu and used it as a defensive weapon to fight police, American militants apparently failed to exploit the advantages of the Japanese technique. Still, self-defense lessons were available in New York City around 1916. In the Hawaiian Islands, classes were first organized for a small group of teachers chaperoned by a Miss Harrison at the Hilo YMCA in 1923. Danzan Ryu jujutsu teacher, Okazaki Seishiro, who taught the classes, spread the practice to other islands and published a much-needed primer of self-defense for women and for girls in 1929.

A British-born jujutsu pioneer, John O'Brien, known as President Roosevelt's first instructor, taught the rudiments of self-defense for girls in a Boston weekly. The illustrations show that with changing courtship rules, flappers of the late 1920s certainly had some use for a few basic jujutsu holds. Even though they were good publicity such comic strips must have been misleading. Few readers probably realized that self-defense implied years of hard training. U.S. judo like Kodokan judo was a male stronghold for many years. Kano, who eventually taught judo to family members, had advocated the practice for girls as long as the conception of the feminine body dictated by contemporary science and eugenic theories were respected. Kano did not want to overtax feminine bodies. At the women's division of the Kodokan or *joshi bu,* formally opened in November 1926, instructors put the stress on health and *kata* learning. The model of the Kodokan reinforced the beliefs of those who thought strength was meant for men and aesthetics for women. During the first half of the 20th century, women practiced judo sporadically. However, although there were no standards for rank promotion, no unity of method or

USJF Archives

Policewoman performing a jujutsu technique, *circa* 1920.

"You want Miss Trimble. She is the smartest worker in my office. This is precisely the type of case she could handle to perfection."
"A woman?" said Mrs. Pett doubtfully.
"A woman in a thousand," said Mr. Surgis.
"A woman in a million." "But physically would a woman be—?"
"Miss Trimble knows more about jiu-jitsu than the Japanese professor who taught her. At one time she was a Strong Woman in small-time vaudeville. She is an expert revolver-shot."

Picadilly Jim, by **Pelham G. Wodehouse, 1917.**

objective, female judoists ignored the problems and joined dojo where they could. During the war, nurses and other members of the military personnel were taught combat techniques while in the camp dojo some women trained with their male counterparts.

Pioneers like June Tegner, Helen Carollo, Ruth Gardner, Ruth Horan, and Phyllis Harper often were judo's goodwill ambassadors. About 1949, Ruth Gardner from Chicago became the first female student to study at Kano's school in Tokyo, Miss Collet from France being the second. Ruth Horan saw judo as fun, as a need, and an excellent physical form of self-protection for anyone who had to use the New York subway system to go to work. Ruth played in a band in Greenwich Village. In 1951, she saw Mel Bruno on *The Arthur Godfrey Show,* then she and her husband decided to take judo classes at the local YMCA on Long Island. In her book, *Judo for Women, a Manual of Self-Defense,* she declared: "Unfortunately there may be times when we are alone and unprotected. Avoiding trouble is the best use of Judo." Defensive judo for women was presented as a service to the community. Women rarely came alone for judo practice. The large majority of them were wives, daughters, or sisters of male judoists. Yamauchi implicitly acknowledged the fact when he stated: "On the mat, there are no mothers, there are no children, there are just judokas." Ruth Horan devoted herself to judo teaching and organizing. Her competence was recognized when she was asked to give a *kata* demonstration at the New York World's Fair.

How to Use Jiu Jitsu for Men and Women, 1943.

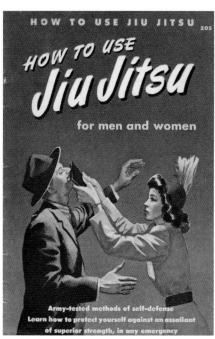

USJF Archives

Helen Carollo was similarly attracted to judo after a public demonstration. In 1941, she joined the Oakland Judo School, where she received instruction based upon the Okazaki method stressing the self-defense aspect of judo. In 1952, she became the first Caucasian woman to be awarded a black belt without going to Japan, a trip she took the year after, eager to train at the Kodokan. Upon her return, a Japanese expert, Fukuda Keiko, accompanied her, as an emissary of the Kodokan.

In 1953, Fukuda was then the highest ranked woman in the world (Kodokan joshi 5th dan). She was instrumental in spreading the methods and spirit of the Joshi Bu dojo. Its motto, "develop one's mind and technique in harmony," became current in American dojo. Fukuda enrolled at the Kodokan in 1935, following Kano's advice to learn judo for health purposes. Until then she had had the very traditional education of young ladies. As the granddaughter of Fukuda Hachinosuke, who taught jujutsu to Kano, she had heard mostly of jujutsu, an art her grandmother herself practiced for self-defense; but as she stated in her book, *Born for the Mat*, she immediately took to judo and never regretted it. Fukuda Keiko and Helen Carollo toured California cities

The Bancroft Library, University of
California, Berkeley

In a conversation with the late Prof. Jigoro Kano, he said to me, "I hope to spread women's judo throughout the world as widely as men's judo. Miss Fukuda, you must pursue the study of judo with this in mind." Naturally, those words of the founder of judo strongly impressed my young mind, and still remain vivid. Since then, I have endeavoured, in my own way to propagate women's judo. Perhaps, because of this effort, Prof. Kano often told men judoists, "If you really want to know true judo, take a look at the methods they use at the Kodokan joshi bu (women's section)." I am very proud of these words which have become a legend in the Kodokan. "Develop one's mind and technique in harmony" is taken as the motto of the women's section, it is also important in men's training. [. . .] The late Prof. Kano's ideal for women's judo was to study randori in parallel with kata. This randori must be done between women. I was instructed only in this manner for the first ten years of my judo study. Judoists in general spend many hours on randori. Although it is also true in women's judo, its characteristic is not to neglect kata while placing the importance on randori. This leads to the realistic methods of self-defense. This results in the increase of confidence in their everyday lives. Those who seriously study judo and master a higher degree of kata, may reach the point of acquiring satori, comparable to that concept of "spiritual enlightment" in Zen Buddhism, possessing a highly trained physique.
Fukuda Keiko, *Born for the Mat*, a Kodokan Kata Textbook for Women, 1973.

Fukuda Keiko.

Courtesy of Fukuda Keiko

USJF Archives

Ruth Gardner, a pioneer of women's judo in the Chicago area.

to give demonstrations stressing the benefits of the physical and mental aspects of judo practice for women, and they worked hard to boost the activity and encourage more women in the sport of judo. Helen Carollo developed the traditionalist point of view according to which the development of skill is hampered by the quest for records, and that women should not participate in tournaments. After her first visit to the mainland U.S., Fukuda stopped in Hawaii and traveled to different countries. She returned to the U.S. in 1966 and started to teach Kodokan judo at Mills College, in Oakland, California.

Fukuda visited many dojo, among them the Senshin Judo Institute, taught by longtime judo pioneer Inouye Tatsuo Ryusei. Inouye's dojo became one of the leaders in *kata* development. Aided by his three daughters Sayuri, Masako, and Kyoko, he contributed to the growth of women's judo. Elizabeth Lee, one of his students, came to be one of the leading *kata* competitors and instructors. She extensively traveled the country to give clinics. Since then she has taught following her motto "be strong, be gentle, be beautiful" in San Francisco and the Bay Area.

During the early 1960s, Phyllis Harper, from Chicago, voiced the leading conception of judo in the States, in the days when the models of the "Feminine Mystique" still prevailed. In an article entitled "Women's judo develops femininity," she stated: "Judo should be ladylike and should embody and exemplify the essence of the gentle way." Takeuchi Kuniko, another emissary from the Kodokan, had a strong influence on women's judo as an educator. But the popularity of women's judo was gradually increased by the achievements and fame of two women with very

"Just for tonight— can't you forget I'm a Black Belt?"

Photo from promotional at the New York Dojo in 1959 with Sensei Gensuke George Yoshida presiding. Guest of Honor Kano Risei and Professor Nakae. In the 1960s, women were part of the judo community.

87ᵗʰ SEMI-ANNUAL PROMOTION MAY 15, 1959

Courtesy of Mel Appelbaum

Rusty Kanokogi.

Courtesy of Rusty Kanokogi

different destinies. Fukuda Keiko played a central role in *kata* teaching and Rusty Kanokogi in competitive judo, two complementary fields which allowed traditions to thrive while a different type of judo was made possible for women on the mat.

The recognition of female judoists' right to compete was long delayed. Some had to fight for it. If in the early 1950s, female judo players were allowed to do so in some countries (e.g., France and Morocco), these isolated attempts were regularly ignored or laughed at. Up until then, women took part in grading contests but were denied the right to compete and obtain official titles. Finally, in the 1960s, in some European countries tournaments were organized for female judo players (West Germany, Switzerland, Austria, Italy, and Great Britain). Judo as a sport no longer was a male territory to be conquered.

On the contrary, female champions claimed equality as a right. Rusty Kanokogi broadened the range of choices available to practitioners when she became the premier ambassador of competitive judo. Her career is underscored by her tenacity as much as by the tensions between sport and womanhood. Her experience as a young judo player further illustrates the assets judo offers as a life principle and an educating tool to turn young people into "useful citizens of society" as Kano explained. Judo and her aunt, Lee Krasner, a celebrated painter, shaped her life. Her social background had given her a special understanding of judo practice for women. As the daughter of an overworked immigrant from the Russian Jewish pale, Rusty Glickman had had to fight her way to survive in Brooklyn streets. Being at the head of a girl's gang, she learned to endure: "Fighting became my sport. It was partly survival, partly love," she declared later.

Rusty Stewart discovered judo in 1954; she was nineteen, a young mother, and had to make ends meet. She was allowed to enter the all-male judo classes at the Brooklyn Central Y provided she taught what she learned to students at the Prospect Park Y where she worked. At first baffled by the mechanics of judo, she came to respect the judo community and to enjoy the grueling training sessions. Her powerful build and her commitment allowed her to defy the rules of separatism. "I was considered an exceptional woman, a woman who played judo like a man." She was soon invited to join the advanced classes of Saiganji Mamaru in Manhattan, where she came of age as a judoist. Energized by her experiences on the mat, Rusty approached the 1961 New York State YMCA championships with a sense of entitlement. Pushing back her short hair and taping her breasts, she used her muscular physique to gatecrash a traditionally male arena. The world of judo blatantly displayed its conservatism. The medal she won was taken away from her. Because she knew the complexity of the judo world, Rusty chose not to fight this decision, knowing she had made her point. In order to prevent any recurrence of the event, the word "male" was surreptitiously added to the titles of all future championships.

BROOKLYN BREEZE...

MR WOLFWHISTLE

NEW YORK MIRROR, WEDNESDAY, DECEMBER 5, 1962

Courtesy of Edgar Allen, Jr.

The high level of expertise reached by Rusty Kanokogi's students inspired famous cartoonist Edgar Allen, Jr.

During the summer, Rusty participated in an international meet aboard *HMS Queen Elizabeth* in New York Harbor. She had to play a man; she won and became an overnight sensation. Among many others, Phyllis Harper wrote to Rusty after this episode. They decided to join forces in order to champion women's judo.

In June 1962, Rusty was a black belt. She left for Japan. After a few classes in the joshi bu dojo she was invited to train in the main dojo. She was soon awarded her second-degree black belt, after a test in front of Kano Risei, the president of the Kodokan. This was unheard of. TV cameras and journalists came to see "the American mother." Back in the States, she continued to teach and train. In 1963, she married a champion supporter of women's judo, Kanokogi Ryohei. They became the highest-ranking American judo couple.

Even though "ladies' classes" continued to be taught nationwide, some martial arts practitioners of the 1970s refused to consider gender as an obstacle. In 1971, the AAU decided to allow women to compete against one another, but with specific "women's rules." Techniques had been modified to avoid body contacts, which almost

FIRST WOMEN'S WORLD JUDO CHAMPIONSHIPS

NEW YORK CITY NOVEMBER 29-30 1980

USJF Archives

Poster of the first Women's World Judo Championships.

Photograph by Lou Di Gesare

eliminated mat work. Such a move taken during the third wave of feminism was untimely and threatening to women, who demanded access to competitive meetings on an equal footing. Rusty and others fought the decision, and eventually standard rules were in use in 1973.

The first AAU national competition for women took place in 1974. The same year the European Judo Union organized an experimental competition in Genoa, Italy. The following year, in Munich, Germany, the first European judo championships for women took place. This decision and the first official titles awarded are all the more symbolic since 1975 was celebrated as the year of women. Nowadays a change in mentalities has occurred. Competition for women is no longer seen as a transgression. In her last book, *Ju no kata,* published in 2005, Fukuda Keiko declared: "Judo training in kata, randori and shiai are the same for men and women." Today 90-year-old Fukuda Keiko is celebrated as one of the last few living disciples of Kano. She is now an American citizen. She is judo's highest-ranked woman and wears a red belt (9th dan), a symbol of her science and resilience. Her mission has been to propagate women's judo, which she has accomplished dutifully over seven decades. She has established her own tournament, the Fukuda Judo Kata Championships, and still teaches three days a week in San Francisco.

Sayaka Matsumoto, silver medalist at the 2000 Junior World Championships in Nabeul, Tunisia.

The first World Championships in New York in 1980, for which Rusty Kanokogi was largely responsible, and essentially the 1982 Paris Championships, radically erased the

Photograph by Bob Willingham

Teri Takemori refereeing at the 2003 World Championships in Osaka. Very few women have gained access to the higher levels as judo referees.

Photograph by Bob Brink

Courtesy of Rusty Kanokogi and Peter Perazio

Patch of the first Women's World Championships. Representing the O in the word judo, the patch was designed after a picture of two of Rusty Kanokogi's students. It was shot by famous ballet photographer Peter Perazio and colored under the recommendations of Rusty's aunt, Lee Krasner, the well-known abstract expressionist and wife of Jackson Pollock.

differences of the past. After the 1988 exhibition at Seoul, a decision was made by the IOC for women's judo to be part of the Olympics. Since 1980, U.S. judo fighters have gained 22 medals during judo world championships. Women have won 10 of them. With new trailblazers and well-trained minds like, among others, twice-Olympian Hillary Wolf or Celita Schutz, a Yale alumna who made her third Olympic appearance in Athens, the prospects for women's judo are more than promising.

A TRUE STORY OF RESPECT

In 1988, the Department of the Navy, through its San Diego Public Affairs office, released an authentic story that possessed all the elements of a true tale of love and war, separation and reunion, a symbol of hope and peace, a modern judo legend.

Al Holtmann, as a Sergeant Major in the U.S. Marine Corps, took part in the 1944 invasion of the isle of Guam, located in the middle of the western Pacific Ocean. In an abandoned old house, on top of a hill, he picked up a notebook written in Japanese. He kept it over the years as a memento of his past adventures, as a sad souvenir of war-torn Guam. Forty years later, after Al had become a renowned judo instructor in the San Diego area in California, he re-discovered the mysterious

Courtesy of Jerry Hays

Al Holtmann.

little diary in an old footlocker as he was packing to move out of his judo school. Al asked one of the members of his judo club, Yoshikai Kyoko, a *nidan* student, to help him find out more about the diary by translating the contents.

Thanks to the diligence of Kyoko and the assistance of relatives and friends in Japan, the family of the unknown author was located. The original copy was sent to the surviving wife. The diary was all the more welcome since it arrived the year of the 50th wedding anniversary of a young couple that war had separated, Yoriko and Takashi Koshimuta.

The text turned out to be full of the daily recollections of a young Japanese husband after he had sent his pregnant wife to Japan in order to shield her from the rigors of the war. Forty years after the discovery of the diary, Al learned from Koshimuta's wife that her gentle husband had been a *nidan* in judo. In times of peace, they could have met on the mat. This anecdote illustrates the level of esteem judo players like Al Holtmann have for Japanese culture. A kind of brotherhood unites the adepts of the method of Kano in the world. They know that fighting goes with respect.

Press release of the San Diego Public Affairs office of the Department of the Navy.

CONCLUSION

J udo is one of the mainstays of Japanese culture in Western countries. Its development in the U.S. highlights the role of Japanese communities willing to recreate in their host countries the cultural roots of their homeland. It is clear that the growth of judo in the U.S. is based upon the dedication of people who devoted themselves to the values designed by Kano. Fractures and splits that occurred resulted from different groups of people willing to promote their personal convictions or interests but references to Kano and to the Kodokan never faded. This close link with Japanese judo is the main characteristic of U.S. judo.

Judo's contributions to society are not restricted to education. Its benefits are not only physical but social and psychological as well. In the field of medicine, a number of academic studies have documented the effectiveness of judo as a complement to traditional medical approaches to treating sickness and disease. Judo has been used in the treatment of asthma, dysmelia, physical handicaps, defective vision, and blindness. Judo has also been used as a complementary system of treatment in rehabilitation programs. In the last few decades, judo has made many inroads into contributing to the health, well-being, and quality of life for many individuals with physical impairments.

The 1st Paralympic Congress and Paralympics Games of Barcelona, in 1992, made the important point that impaired athletes are recognized overall for what they can do and for who they are, elite athletes. During the Paralympics in Athens, in 2004, U.S. elite players Lori Pierce, Scott Moore, and Kevin Szott were strong enough to bring Olympic medals home. Becoming part of a judo dojo allows visually impaired individuals to get out of their specialized schools, to gain initiative, self-confidence, and the ability to handle risks, to meet other people, and to compete on the same level as others. Doing so, they fight against isolation, learn to respect others, and socialize. Judo is therefore an important mechanism of integration.

The guidelines of judo have been relatively widely used in psychotherapy. One study in the *American Journal of Psychotherapy* documents how judo tactics can be applied to conflict-solving strategies during psychotherapy.

146

Many other reports demonstrate the benefits of judo practice as a method to bring meaning and self-esteem to people from many walks of life, including children and adults, adolescent delinquents, physically and mentally handicapped and emotionally disturbed individuals, and many others. The basic principles of judo have been used to understand, analyze, explain, and predict behavior in psychology, education, medicine, anthropology, economics, business, and other fields. In the business world, more and more professionals are attracted by what is known as "corporate judo." This refers to the ability to pursue emerging opportunities while avoiding direct confrontation with competition, the flexibility to change course when required and yield when faced with an impending defeat, and the exploitation of leverage to turn competitors' strengths into weaknesses.

The contributions of judo to society are numerous and can be extended to many other fields. The value of Kano's method goes much beyond its confines as a sport, and makes a substantial contribution to the livelihood of many people. In the United States, one of the most popular and effective methods of communication techniques used by police and law enforcement agencies across the country is known as "verbal judo." Verbal Judo or Tactical Communication is part of a top-rated law enforcement communication course in the U.S., with over 125,000 officers from over 700 departments as graduates. It involves the gentle art of persuasion that redirects the behavior of others with words, and generates voluntary compliance. It enables officers to further preserve law and order, while maintaining their own and the public's safety by using appropriate presence and words as force options. It is a philosophy that prepares officers to be ready in every verbal encounter, to listen and speak more effectively, to engage others through empathy, and to avoid the most common conversational disasters. It is, of course, the principle of judo itself, using the energy of others to master situations.

The Verbal Judo course teaches a philosophy of how to look creatively at conflicts, offering specific, powerful, and usable strategies to resolve tense situations. The main goals are conflict management, enhanced professionalism, and increased efficiency. Its benefits have been discussed in newspapers, magazines, and other publication sources all around the U.S. In addition to its popularity in peace and law enforcement officers' training, judo principles and techniques have been taught in schools, helping students manage conflict and tension, and in businesses, allowing employees to work and function more productively and effectively. Similar techniques have also been used by lawyers in the courtroom.

Judo's contributions to social problems do not stop with law enforcement, however. Many judo instructors sacrifice their time, effort, and expertise to help keep kids off the streets, and to turn around lives gone haywire. At the Detroit YMCA in Michigan, judo classes under the instruction of Paul Singleton focus on students who are victims of urban violence, rape, juvenile delinquency, and drugs. Students find options for their life other than living in gangs, or on the streets. By plunging into judo practice, they get back on track in their lives with school, work, and family. Similar great work in the communities goes on at the Simi Valley Boys and Girls Club in Southern California. Under the tutelage of instructor Ray Tinaza, judo helps troubled teens turn their lives around.

Another unique judo program that serves its community is used by the Atlanta Judo Academy, headed by Bob Byrd and Leo White. The students in this program had been arrested for minor crimes like smoking marijuana, underage drinking, shoplifting, or theft. A state court judge gave them an option: go to jail, spend more than $1,000 on probation fees, or take judo. The program is turning lives around. Judo teaches these first-time non-violent crime offenders valuable lessons about discipline, anger management, respect for themselves, and respect for others. So far, the program has been extremely successful, with very low relapse rates.

Judo values and mechanics are recognized by the general public. Many builders of the American nation are known as judo practitioners. From President Theodore Roosevelt in the past to today's Colorado Senator and ex-judo Olympian, Ben Nighthorse Campbell, many were influenced or shaped by the practice of the Japanese hand-to-hand method, by the teaching of the desire to fulfill one's aspirations in respect of others. The values promoted by Kano and his followers are identified in the behavior of people who acquired their philosophy notably through judo practice. Jeremy Glick, who showed his courage on board United Flight 93, on September 11, 2001, was one of them. Judo, as a sport and as a principle of life, has obviously built for many community members a high threshold of endurance to adversity. It has certainly helped many men and women, in ways that Kano probably only dreamed of.

PEANUTS © by Charles Schultz

Judo has come a
long way.
It is now part
of the world of
American icons.

PALMARES

Junior World Championships Medalists

1994
Hilary Wolf, Gold, −48 kg

2000
Sayaka Matsumoto, Silver, −48 kg

2004
Ronda Rousey, Gold, −63 kg

Olympic Medalists

1964
James Bregman, Bronze, −80 kg

1976
Allen Coage, Bronze, +93 kg

1984
Eddie Liddie, Bronze, −60 kg

1984
Robert Berland, Silver, −86 kg

1988
Kevin Asano, Silver, −60 kg

1988
Lynn Roethke, Silver, −61 kg

1988
Mike Swain, Bronze, −71 kg

1988
Margaret Castro, Bronze, +72 kg

1992
Jason Morris, Silver, −78 kg

1996
Jimmy Pedro, Bronze, −71 kg

2004
Jimmy Pedro, Bronze, −73 kg

Junior World Championships Medalists

1965
James Bregman, Bronze, −80 kg

1980
M. Lewis, Bronze, −48 kg

1980
Christine Penick, Bronze, −66 kg

1980
B. Fest, Bronze, Open

1982
Eve Aronoff, Bronze, −56 kg

1982
Margaret Castro, Silver, +72kg

1983
Robert Berland, Bronze, −86 kg

1984
Darlen Anya, Silver, −48 kg

1984
Darlen Anya, Silver, −48 kg

1984
Ann Marie Burns, Gold, −56 kg

1985
Mike Swain, Silver, −71 kg

Kevin Asano, Bronze, −60 kg

1987
Lynn Roethke, Silver, −61 kg

1987
Mike Swain, Gold, −71 kg

1989
Mike Swain, Silver, −71 kg

1991
James Pedro, Bronze, −65 kg

1991
Joey Wanag, Silver, −86 kg

1993
Jason Morris, Bronze, −78 kg

1993
Liliko Ogasawara, Silver, −66 kg

1995
James Pedro, Bronze, −71 kg

1995
Liliko Ogasawara, Bronze, −66 kg

1997
Brian Olson, Bronze, −86 kg

1999
Jimmy Pedro, Gold, −73 kg

List of IJF A Referees

Dr. Melvin M. Appelbaum, Ph.D.
Dr. Sachio Ashida, Ph.D.
Dr. Gary C. Berliner, M.D.
Dr. Martin L. Bregman, Ph.D.
Richard J. Celotto
Kwijoon K. Chi
Young Nam Chung
Thomas T. Dalton, Esq.*
Roy T. Englert, Esq.
Hector E. Estevez
Robert S. Fukuda
Richard M. Hugh
Jongoon Kim
Dr. Eichi K. Koiwai, M.D.
R. David Long
Dr. David R. Matsumoto, Ph.D.
Frank Morales, Jr.
Dr. Kei Narimatsu, D.D.S.
Hayward H. Nishioka
John Osako*
Noboru Saito
Russell L. Scherer
Thomas S. Seabasty
David L. Smith, Esq.
Gaile L. Spadin
Tae Jing Suk
J. Teri Takemori
Gary H. Takemoto
Fletcher Thornton
George S. Uchida*

*deceased

Officers & Executive Committee

President	**Noboru Saito** 139 Roth Boulevard Clawson, MI 48017
1st Vice President	**Vaughn T. Imada** 1209 Capri Drive Campbell, CA 95008
2nd Vice President	**Julie A. Koyama** 3106 N.E. 11th Avenue Portland, OR 97212
Secretary	**Vicki C. Trent,** Esq. 175 Red Rock Way, K-107 San Francisco, CA 94131
Treasurer	**Neil J. Simon** 17340 W. 12 Mile Road Southfield, MI 48076
Chairperson of the Board of Examiners	**Yoshisada Yonezuka** 107 South Avenue West Cranford, NJ 07016
Corporate Counsel	**Richard H. Muller**, Esq. 5806 S.E. 41st Avenue Portland, OR 97202
Advisor to the President	**Robert C. Brink**, Esq. 1525 East Tudor Road Anchorage, AK 99507
Executive Director	**Robert S. Fukuda** P.O. Box 338 Ontario, OR 97914

http://www.usjf.com/

SOURCES AND FURTHER READING

Amateur Athletic Union of U.S., *1963 Official AAU Judo Handbook*,
New York, AAU, 1963, 288 pp.

Applegate, Rex, Lieutenant Colonel, *Kill or Get Killed, Manhandling
Techniques for the Police and the Military*, Harrisburg, Pa.,
The Military Service Publishing Co., 1958 (1943), 332 pp.

Arima, Sumitomo, *Judo, Japanese Physical Culture, Being a Further
Exposition of Jujitsu and Similar Arts by Professor Sumitomo
Arima*, Tokyo, Mitsumura, 1908, 137 pp.

Atkinson, Linda, *Women in the Martial Arts, a New Spirit Rising*, New York,
Dodd, Mead & Co., 1983, 181 pp.

Blanchard, Robert G., *The Mechanics of Judo, Analytical Studies of
Selected Standing Techniques*, Rutland, Vt., Charles E. Tuttle
Co., 1961, 134 pp.

Brousse, Michel, *Le Judo, son Histoire, ses Succès*, préface de Jacques
Rogge, Président du CIO Genève, Liber, 2002, 212 pp.

Brousse, Michel, and Matsumoto, David, *Judo, a sport and a way of
life*, Seoul, International Judo Federation, 1999, 164 pp.

Cosneck, Bernard J., *American Combat Judo*, New York, Sentinel
Books Pub. Inc., 1944, 125 pp.

Draeger, Donn, *The Martial Arts and Ways of Japan: Volume 1,
Classical Bujutsu, Volume II, Classical Budo, Volume III, Modern
Bujutsu & Budo*, New York, Weatherhill, 1983 (1974).

Fukuda Keiko, *Born for the Mat, a Kodokan Textbook for Women,
Judo*, San Francisco, Ca., Private edition, 1976 (1973), 140 pp.

Fukuda Keiko, *Ju No Kata, a Kodokan Judo Textbook*, North Atlantic
Books, Berkeley, Ca., 2004, 200 pp.

Gardner, Ruth B., *Judo for the Gentle Woman*, Rutland, Vt., Charles E.
Tuttle Co., 1971, 141 pp.

Hancock H. Irving, *Jiu-Jitsu Combat Tricks. Japanese Feats of Attack
and Defence in Personal Encounter*, New York, Putman's Sons,
1905, 152 pp.

Hancock, H. Irving, and Higashi Katsukuma, *The Complete Kano Jiu-
Jitsu (Judo)*, New York, Dover, 1961 (1905), 500 pp.

Harrington, Patricia, *Judo, a Pictorial Manual*, Rutland, Vt., Charles
Tuttle Co., 1992, 280 pp.

Harrison, E. J., *The Fighting Spirit of Japan and Other Stories*, London,
Foulsham, [1912], 250 pp.

Helm, Dennis et al, *2000 Years Jujitsu and Kodokan Judo,* Rockford, The Illinois Judo Association, 1991, 116 pp.

Kano Jigoro, *Judo (Jujutsu),* Board of Tourist Industry, Japanese Government Railways, s. l., 1937, 70 pp.

Kobayashi, Kiyoshi, and Sharp, Harold E., *The Sport of Judo as Practiced in Japan,* Rutland, Vt., Charles E. Tuttle Co., 1972 (1956), 104 pp.

Kodokan, *Judo by the Kodokan,* Osaka, Nunoi Shobo Co., 1961, 152 pp.

Kodokan, supervised by, *Kano Jigoro Taikei, vol. 12, Collection of Photographs,* Hon no Tomo Sha, Tokyo, 1988, 221 pp.

Kuwashima, T. S., and Welch, A. R., *Judo, Forty-one Lessons in the Modern Science of Jiu-Jitsu,* London, Putnam & Company Ltd., 1951 (1938), 156 pp.

Leyshon, Glynn A., *The History of Judo in Canada,* Gloucester, Ontario, Judo Canada, 1997, 188 pp.

Linck, Samuel, *Combat Jiu Jitsu for Offense and Defense,* Portland, USA, Stevens-Ness Law Publishing, 1943, 126 pp.

Lindsay, Thomas, and Kano Jigoro, "Jiujutsu, the Old Samurai Art of Fighting Without Weapons," in *Transactions of the Asiatic Society of Japan,* Vol. XVI, 1889, pp. 192–205.

Lowell, Frederick Paul, *The Way to Better Judo,* New York, Exposition Press, a Banner Book, 1952, 248 pp.

Maekawa, M., and Y. Hasegawa, "Studies on Jigoro Kano, Significance of His Ideals of Physical Education and Judo," in *Bulletin of the Association for the Scientific Studies on Judo,* Kodokan, Tokyo, Report 2, 1963, pp. 1–12.

Maruyama, Sanzo, *Dai Nihon Judo Shi,* Tokyo, Kodokan, 1939, 1170 pp.

Matsumoto, David, *An Introduction to Kodokan Judo, History and Philosophy,* Tokyo, Hon no Tomosha, 1996, 316 pp.

Matsumoto, Yoshizo, compiled by, *Kano Jigoro Chosakushu,* Tokyo, Ed. Satsukishobo, 1983, vol. I, II, III.

Nakabayashi, Sadaki, Nagao, Hikaru, Okamura, Henry, and Harper, Paul, *Judo,* New York, Sterling Publishing Co., 1966, 128 pp.

Nelson, Randy F., and Whitaker, Katherine C., *The Martial Arts, An Annotated Bibliography,* New York, Garland Publishing, Inc., 1988, 456 pp.

Nishioka, Hayward, *Judo, Heart and Soul,* Santa Clarita, Ohara Pub., 1999, 256 pp.

Nishioka, Hayward, and West, James, *The Judo Textbook in Practical Application*, Santa Clarita, Ca., Ohara Publications, Inc., 1979, 192 pp.

Ogasawara, Nagayasu, *Textbook of Judo*, Montvale, N.J., Kokushi Dojo Inc., 1988, 274 pp.

Saint-Hilaire, Russ, *Pioneers of American Jujitsu before WWII*, West Hartfort, Ct., 2004, 128 pp.

Smith, Robert W., *A Complete Guide to Judo, Its Story and Practice*, Rutland, Vt., Charles E. Tuttle Co., 249 pp.

Smith, Robert W., *Martial Musings, a Portryal of Martial Arts in the 20th Century,* Via Media Publishing Company, Erie, Pa., 1999, 390 pp.

Svinth, Joseph R., *Getting a Grip: Judo in the Nikkei Communities of the Pacific Northwest, 1900–1950,* EJMAS, Seattle, Wa., 2003, 300 pp.

Tegner, Bruce, *Bruce Tegner's Complete Book of Judo*, New York, Bantam, 1970 (1967), 256 pp.

Training Division of Aeronautics, U.S. Navy, *Hand-to-Hand Combat*, Annapolis, United States Naval Institute, 1943, 228 pp.

U.S. Marine Corps, *Hand-to-Hand Combat*, McDonald, Ohio, Hillcrest, 1957, 60 pp.

Waterhouse, David, "Kano Jigoro and the Beginnings of the Judo Movement," *Proceedings of Toronto Symposium*, Toronto University, 1982, pp. 168–178.

Watson, Brian N., *The Father of Judo, a Biography of Jigoro Kano*, Tokyo, Kodansha International, 2000, 212 pp.

Yerkow, Charles, *Judo Katas Fundamentals of Throwing and Mat Techniques (Nage-no-Kata and Katame-no-Kata)*, Englewood Cliffs, N.J., Prentice-Hall, Inc., 1961 (1955), 163 pp.

Yerkow, Charles, *Modern Judo, Volume I. Basic Technique, Modern Judo, Volume II. Advanced Technique.* Harrisburg, The Military Service Publishing Co., 1951 (1942).

Yerkow, Charles, *Sport Judo*, Harrisburg, Stackpole and Heck, Inc., 1950, 162 pp.

Yoffie, David B., and Kwak, Mary, *Judo Strategy*, Harvard Business School Press, Boston, 2001, 239 pp.

DAVID MATSUMOTO

Photograph by Bob Willingham

David Matsumoto is an internationally acclaimed author and psychologist. He received his B.A. from the University of Michigan in 1981 with High Honors. He subsequently earned his M.A. and Ph.D. in psychology from the University of California at Berkeley. He is currently Professor of Psychology and Director of the Culture and Emotion Research Laboratory at San Francisco State University, where he has been since 1989. He has studied culture, emotion, and social interaction and communication for 20 years, and has written over 250 works in these areas. His books include well-known titles such as *Culture and Psychology: People Around the World; The Intercultural Adjustment Potential of Japanese,* and *The Handbook of Culture and Psychology.* His newest book, *The New Japan,* has received national and international acclaim. He is the recipient of many awards and honors in the field of psychology, including being named a G. Stanley Hall lecturer by the American Psychological Association. He gives speeches to audiences all around the world and serves as a consultant to many international businesses, especially those dealing with intercultural training.

David Matsumoto is also a world-renowned judo coach and official. He holds a 6th degree black belt in judo, a Class A Coaching Certificate from USA Judo, and a Class A International Referee License from the International Judo Federation. He is the head instructor of the East Bay Judo Institute, one of the U.S.A.'s top competitive dojos. He is the recipient of the 1999 U.S. Olympic Committee's Developmental Coach of the Year Award in Judo, the 2001 U.S. Judo Federation's Senior and Junior Female Coach of the Year Award, and an acclamation from the City and County of Honolulu, HI, in 1977. Under his leadership as the Director of Development for USA Judo from 1996 to 2000, the U.S. claimed its first gold medal in 12 years at the 1999 World Judo Championships, and qualified a full team of athletes for the 2000 Sydney Olympic Games. In the third year of his directorship, American judo athletes stood on the medal podium at international competitions a total of 124 times. His personal students have distinguished themselves by obtaining medals in national and international competition over 200 times in the past 18 years under his tutelage, including a silver medal at the 2000 International Judo Federation World Junior Judo Championships by his daughter, Sayaka. He is the author of *The History and Philosophy of Kodokan Judo* and co-author of *Judo: A Sport and a Way of Life*.

MICHEL BROUSSE

M ichel Brousse is a sport historian and a judo expert. He graduated from the National Institute of Sports in Paris, France. He earned his thesis from the Faculty of Science of Sports and Physical Education at Bordeaux University, where he is currently professeur agrégé teaching the cultural history of sport and didactics of judo. His works include *Les Origines du Judo en France, Histoire d'un Culture Sportive, de la Fin du XIXᵉ Siècle aux Années 1950,* Presses Universitaires de Bordeaux, 2005; *Le Judo, son Histoire, ses Succès,* préface de Jacques Rogge, Président du CIO, Liber, 2002.

Photograph by Bob Willingham

He is the author of various articles in French, English, Spanish, and Portuguese. He has made guest addresses to professionals on the history of sports and on the didactics of judo or physical education in France, the U.S.A., Brazil, Korea, Great Britain, Morocco, Spain, and Portugal. From 1996 to 2002, he was a member of a Ministry of Education study group to write the first national syllabus for high school physical education.

Michel Brousse is a 6th degree black belt. From 1969 to 1981, he was a member of the French judo team (50 selections). His best results are: three times European champion, in Berlin, 1969, in Bordeaux, 1970, and in Naples, 1971; twice Military World champion: under 93 kg, Open class, in Rio de Janeiro, 1974; 3rd in Seniors national championships under 93 kg, 1973; 5th Open class, 1974. He also won the gold in Pecs tournament, Hungary, in 1977, and the bronze in the 1979 Paris Open.

Michel Brousse was a coach for the European Judo Union and for the International Judo Federation. Over the years, he has run judo clinics for national teams and coaches in France, Norway, Iceland, Denmark, Spain, Portugal, Venezuela, and the U.S.A. In the late 1970s, in Paris, he was head coach and supervisor of a sport and study section where he was lucky enough to have brilliant young students who later became stars on the judo world scene. Among them were Pascal Tayot (Olympic medalist), Christophe Gagliano (Olympic medalist), and Bertrand Amoussou (French judo team then five times jujutsu world champion). Michel Brousse was nominated official researcher for the International Judo Federation in 1998. With David Matsumoto, he is the co-author of *Judo: A Sport and a Way of Life.* He was media commissioner and spokesperson for the International Judo Federation during the Sydney Olympic Games, 2001 Munich and 2003 Osaka World Championships, and Athens Olympic Games.

CREDITS

The authors and publisher have endeavored to get permission to use all the illustrations included in this book. There were some cases where copyrights have expired, the original publishing company is no longer in existence, or the original owner is deceased. Credits are presented in alphabetical order and followed by the page number.

Bernard Pariset 106; Black Belt Magazine 88, 101, 115; Black Cat © Lorne-Harvey Publications 105; Bob Brink 144; Bob Willingham 128, 129, 130, 133, 135, 136, 143, 154, 155; The Buddhist Churches of America 34; Dave Enslow 98; David Finch 124, 125, 126, 127; Edgar Allen, Jr. 142; Emilio Bruno 42, 62, 63, 83, 90, 91, 92; Fukuda Keiko 139; Fukusawa Akio 81; Georges Arrington 32; Harold Yamada 35; The Hirasake National Resource Center of the Japanese American National Museum 66, 67, 73; The IOC / Olympic Museum Collection 15, 123, 127, 131; James Bregman 86, 118, 122; The Japanese Americans Centennial Committee 32, 33, 36, 58; Jason Morris 128; The Jerome Robbins Dance Division of the New York Public Library 28; Jerry Hays 70, 82, 145; Kiku Masamune 10; The Kodokan Institute 4, 5, 6, 7, 9, 10, 11, 12, 14, 16, 17, 19, 23, 24, 27, 28, 29, 34, 38, 39, 41, 43, 52, 53, 55, 56, 57, 59, 98, 108; Lou Di Gesare 143; Marion Brousse 64, 94; The Mary Hill Museum of Art 24; Mel Appelbaum 60, 140; PEANUTS © by United Feature Syndicate, Inc. 104, 148; Playboy Magazine 103; Popular Science 105; Ringling Bros. and Barnum & Bailey 18; Rusty Kanokogi 141; Rusty Kanokogi and Peter Perazio 144; Sakai Yoshitaro 119; The Todd-MacLean Physical Culture Collection 25; Tribune Media Services 101; The University of California, Berkeley 50, 69, 71, 72, 77, 139; The University of Washington Press 75; USJF Archives 19, 20, 21, 22, 25, 26, 29, 30, 31, 37, 40, 43, 44, 45, 47, 48, 49, 65, 78, 79, 84, 85, 87, 89, 93, 96, 99, 100, 102, 107, 110, 111, 112, 113, 114, 121, 137, 138, 140, 142; Victory Comics 112.

The following pages contain illustrations without source citations: 8, 13, 15, 21, 26, 39, 46, 51, 54, 61, 68, 69, 74, 75, 86, 95, 96, 97, 106, 107, 109, 114, 116, 117, 120, 123, 129, 140, 141, 145

DONORS

Acknowledgment is given to our sponsors who contributed to the publication cost.
This book could not have been edited without their assistance.

Donors of $2,000 or more

Robert C. Brink, Esq.
M. David Conlan
Teruyuki Miura
Noboru & Freya Saito

Donors of $1,000 or more

Leslie E. Stewart

Donors of $500 or more

In Honor of Edward & Grace Akiya
Elizabeth Balch
In Honor of James Cornforth
Sanjoy Ghosh
Toshio Ichinoe
In Honor of Mitsuho & Helen Kimura
Michigan Judo Development Association
Yoshisada Yonezuka

Donors of $200 or more

Alan K. Honda
Vaughn & Phyllis Imada
Garrett C. Keais
Konan Judo Yudanshakai
Dr. James M. Lally
Daniel J. Mitoraj
Dr. Chris J. Mitsuoka
Jim S. & Fumi Onchi
Koji Oshima

Donors of $100 or more

American Judo-Hapkido Institute, John Beluschak, Bothell Judo—Joe Butler, Wilson A. Burgess, Chuka Yudanshakai, Dr. Richard A. Cirone, Jack W. Ferrill, In Honor of Hiro Fujimoto, The Fujiokas, Robert Fukuda, In Honor of Dick Fukuyama, Gambaru Yudanshakai, Ronald E. Hansen, Demetris Haritos, Mrs. Rumiko Hatano, Bret K. Holmes, Alan & Sandy Honda, David & Myles Honda, Intermountain Yudanshakai, Jerry P. Jeziorski, Timothy J. Jordan, Esq., Dr. Ricardo G. Joseph, M.D., Joseph S. Kajita, Rusty & Ryohei Kanokogi, Donald A. Kelley, Brett M. Layton, Wallace M. Luster, Bert A. Mackey, Jr., John & Louise Mackey, Nidal F. Makki, Guy Matsuoka, Tawni McBee, Howard J. Nam, Wataru & Reiko Namba, Dr. Kei Narimatsu, Northwest Judo Yudanshakai, Anthony R. Owed, Richard E. Petherbridge, Philip Porter, Jack & Mary Rogers, Brian Ruhoff, Amy & June Saito, Thomas J. Sheehan, Tone Shimizu, Ed & Joan Shiosaki, Shufu Judo Yudanshakai, Stanley Sochanek, Robert Treat—Southside Dojo, Michael Stebbins, Gordan Sugimoto, Jeffrey T. Takeda, James H. Takemori, George Y. Tsubota, In Honor & Memory of a Half Century of USJF Senseis, Gerald P. Uyeno, Gerald E. Wee, Dr. Bruce E. Wilson, M.D., Paul Yoshimune—Pacific Judo

Donors of $50 or more

Joseph A. Ahern, Kwijoon K. Chi, Kenneth Davis, Karen M. DuPage, Deborah L. Fergus, Vernon D. Johnson, William D. Kennings, Zoltan Kovacs, Thomas Koyama Family, Michael & Sharon Landstreet, Rene Leidelmeyer, Richard H. Muller Esq., Jim, Alex, & Tara Murray, Nagayasu Ogasawara, Susan S. Oles, Richard E. Petherbridge, Neal Takamoto, Howard S. Takata, Jack M. Turrentine, Harold A. Yamada, Sam Zeoli

United States Judo Federation

Celebrating 50 Years of Excellence & Tradition

The following is a list of some of the scholarships and grants we offer our members:

Keiko Fukuda Judo Scholarship

George C. Balch Education Judo Scholarship

Tamo Kitaura Referee Grant

Elizabeth Lee Judo Scholarship

Athlete-Scholar of the Year Award

Contact our National Office for more information, forms, and contact info for local representatives from one of our many Yudanshakais: 50th State Judo Association • Arizona Judo Yudanshakai • Central Coast Judo Association • Chicago Judo Black Belt Association • Chuka Judo Yudanshakai • Daiheigen Judo Yudanshakai • Florida Judo Yudanshakai • Florida State Judo Yudanshakai • Ganbaru Judo Yudanshakai • Hawaii State Judo Association • Hokka Judo Yudanshakai • Hudson Judo Yudanshakai • Intermountain Judo Yudanshakai • Judo Black Belt Association of Hawaii • Konan Judo Yudanshakai • Nanka Judo Yudanshakai • Niagara Judo Yudanshakai • Northwest Judo Yudanshakai • Pacific Southwest Judo Association • Rokushu Judo Yudanshakai • San Joaquin Valley Judo Association • Shinnanbu Judo Yudanshakai • Shufu Judo Yudanshakai • Southern Pacific Judo Association

United States Judo Federation
National Office
P. O. Box 338
Ontario, OR 97914-0338

Phone: (541) 889-8753
FAX: (541) 889-5836
FAX #2: (413) 502-4983
www.usjf.com

Hudson Judo Yudanshakai

Congratulates $USJF$ on their 50th Anniversary

Great Respect is given to the USA's

Original Judo development organization

HUDSON JUDO YUDANSHAKAI

President	Yoshisada Yonezuka
1st VP	Mamoru Shimamoto
2nd VP	Rusty Kanokogi
Treasurer	Joseph Ahern
Secretary	Robin Rosenfield
Registration	Liza McKay